RIGHT TO A FUTURE

The Native Peoples of Canada

BY JOHN MELLING

PUBLISHED JOINTLY BY

THE ANGLICAN CHURCH OF CANADA
AND
THE UNITED CHURCH OF CANADA

Cover design:
William Turnbull

Printed in Canada
by T. H. Best Printing Company Limited, Don Mills, Ontario

Foreword

The publication of this book represents the first venture which the combined Churches of Canada have made into the field of literature on the Canadian Indian-Eskimo concern.

The author, Professor John Melling, originally submitted his manuscript to an interdepartmental committee of the Anglican Church of Canada, which shared it with sister committees in other denominations. Their interest and favourable reaction encouraged the Anglican committee to invite participation in its publication as a co-operative venture. Accordingly, the book is now offered to the Canadian public as a statement on an important issue in our national life. It appears most appropriately during the Centennial Year when concerns of this nature deserve to be examined with seriousness and appreciation. The following Churches and organizations commend this book to the members of their respective communions and to the Canadian public:

> The Anglican Church of Canada
> The Baptist Convention of Ontario and Quebec
> The Canadian Council of Churches
> The Conference of Mennonites in Canada
> The Indian-Eskimo Association of Canada
> The Lutheran Council in Canada
> The Presbyterian Church in Canada
> The Roman Catholic Church
> The Salvation Army
> The Religious Society of Friends
> The United Church of Canada

Preface

For some years now, particularly since World War II, a combination of factors has both drastically altered the situation of Canada's native peoples and also brought it from a peripheral to a more central place on the Canadian scene. It has become abundantly clear that both government and Church need to reassess and refocus their concern and responsibilities for and with these peoples if creative steps are to be taken to meet present realities.

Dean Melling, from a background of disciplined study and extensive personal contact, both of these arising from a deep human concern, has written *Right to a Future: The Native Peoples of Canada* in which many penetrating insights are clearly evident. In so doing he has rendered a great service to native Canadians, to government agencies and to many Church bodies, for this book provides a much needed source of information for the reassessment and refocusing which are so urgently required. It is to be hoped that his efforts will not be wasted but that they will, in fact, help stimulate much thought and action as we seek to develop more creative attitudes, relationships and policies in this area of our country's life.

EDWARD W. SCOTT
The Bishop of Kootenay

TABLE OF CONTENTS

Introduction

This book is written in the belief that Canadians should pause in the midst of their centennial pride and consider their fellow-citizens of native background. It is to be hoped that they will use the pause for some study and discussion and that this book will be helpful for that purpose.

If there *is* a discussion, this book will not sentimentalize it with a lament or paralyse it with scientific predictions. It is written with a *commitment*: to help the native peoples of Canada in ways consistent with membership in the Church. It has therefore to consider what the human rights of the native peoples may be while avoiding a prejudgment of what their culturally-shaped needs actually are. It tries to bring Church thinking into touch with social science, though without simulating the neutral posture of science. It runs the risk of disownment by science and the Church.

It runs the risk of disownment by others too. Government will think itself unkindly assessed in its work on behalf of the native peoples. Métis and Eskimos, if they get to know of the book, will consider their case to be under-represented here. Indians may conclude I am no friend of theirs because, though I do not say so, I may be thought to imply that they are destined to disappear without trace into our urban-industrial salariat, only retaining their reserves as desirable cottage lots now expanded (or contracted) to a new sort of status symbol.

These risks are integral to the present enterprise. In a small book one can only say part of what ought to be said; because of the commitment one has to say certain things that some people will think ought not to be said. In any case, on such a subject as Canadian native affairs, one cannot please everyone.

This book is not the result of my own research. It does, however, use the research findings of others, including certain unpublished findings. The only writers to whose research I know I am indebted who are not referred to in the text are Professors Hawthorn, Jamieson and Belshaw, authors of the epoch-making work on *The Indians of British Columbia*. I have looked at all this research in the light of my own five years in Indian work, which brought me vivid, though too brief, experiences in scores, if not hundreds, of native communities from sea to sea.

J. M.

20th November, 1966.

SECTION I

CHAPTER I

The Churches and Politics

Those Canadians who are deeply concerned about the prospects of the country's Indians and Eskimos would be hard put at this moment to decide whether to be hopeful or apprehensive. On the one hand, there is considerable evidence of a fresh dawn in Indian-Eskimo affairs. On the other hand, the dawn could peter out, surviving only in memory as a false dawn. There must be many of our native peoples in Canada today who are agitated by the thought: But will the new day come? Since none of us knows, the present is a critically important moment for facing the question: Is there anything we can do to ensure a new deal for those whom we call the "First Canadians"—even though most of us habitually put them last?

The question faces us not only as Canadian citizens but as members of the Churches. As democrats we shall naturally want to insist on just policies for Canadian native affairs. This will also be part of our Christian responsibility. But for the rest, as Christians, we shall be less concerned about affairs than about persons, and less concerned about the Indian as an Indian, or the Eskimo as an Eskimo, than about both of them as human beings. Likewise, we shall recognize that these people are confined to a situation so generally unequal with our own that, as Christians, we shall want them to receive an unequal share of our time and effort.

There is, however, a tension between our democratic way of judging things and our Christian way. In the mechanics of democracy, majorities matter. Small and weak minorities tend to be overlooked. But in the sight of the Churches, minorities matter. If they are small and weak, they matter more. An identical attention to each and all would not be Christian charity but rather the ballotbox principle by which each counts as one and no one counts as more than one. Somehow, Church folk must help diminish the gap

3

between the morality of Jesus and the mathematics of democratic politics. Two hundred thousand "registered" Indians, at least sixty thousand Métis, and ten thousand Eskimos must not be measured against nineteen million whites in order to see things in perspective. What gives perspective is the need these people are suffering—the same need their fathers and forefathers suffered, a need that still impoverishes the present generation. The least important consideration is head-counting. That within thirty-five years the native peoples will number one million will never be so important as that over a quarter of a million of them need a better life today.

Bringing Christian insights to bear on civic responsibility is part of general Christian practice. In particular, these insights should include knowing *when* to do *what*. Though we should always be considering what the body of society needs for the sake of its health, we should also have a sense of "times and seasons" and recognize what is most important to be done *now*. We shall not, however, know what our characteristically Christian tasks are at this moment unless we strengthen or maintain two characteristically Christian attitudes. First, "the enthusiasm of humanity"—enthusiasm for humanity as it ought to be. Second, a sense of fellowship with other human beings, such as cuts across or cuts away the worldly divisions of class or creed or race. The record of the relations of Canadian whites with the native peoples does not assure us that Christian conscience has been as widespread, as sensitive and as informed as it should have been. These pages at least will provide much evidence that any time during the last century would have been late enough to do something positively Christian through Church or State to halt or reverse the desperate deterioration in the lives of our neighbours, the Indians, Métis and Eskimos.

The need for action cannot be gainsaid. If we do too little for too long, history catches us up and forces those challenges upon us to which our consciences have been too slow to respond. In what concerns the relations of whites and the coloured peoples of the world —people yellow and black as well as brown—the compulsions of politics are already evident. Today our own Indians demonstrate in Kenora, as yesterday American Negroes demonstrated in Selma and as next year Rhodesian Africans may demonstrate in Bulawayo. Expediency as well as principle, the crassest material considerations as well as spiritual concern, proclaim the ripeness of the present time for neighbourly deeds between the races at home and abroad. Those of us who seek reconciliation with people of a different colour here at home should act as directly as possible; where that cannot be, our deeds must be delegated—to government or to the home missions of our Churches. Above all, they should be such deeds as the native peoples have been yearning for us to perform and such therefore as they can understand, can co-operate with, and harmonize with their own sense of values. Of one thing, however, we must beware: if the Indians and Eskimos have suffered for generations a stifling kind of neglect, we must not now smother them with that kind of attention that continues to depress their own efforts. In helping our neighbours, their sense of need, their purposes, and their spontaneities should shape the end we cherish for them.

In a situation of social need such as now confronts our native peoples—a situation too grave to be remedied by one party or agency alone—it is always difficult to know or to state precisely what is the responsibility of those who are to be helped, what the responsibility of the Churches, and what the responsibility of the government. That those who are to be helped should be active and resourceful in their own behalf and set the objectives at which their efforts aim we have already seen. But where does self-help end and received help begin? In a situation of the kind we are discussing, the received help will have to be of different sorts, physical and financial and administrative and moral and spiritual. And just as a helper (or self-helper) is helpless to remove unaided a serious social evil, so a single type of help is inadequate to the same task. A famous colonial administrator once said: "Let us not give the people cause to complain that, when they asked for bread, we gave them the vote." Equally we could say: Let us not give the people cause to complain that, when they asked for the vote, we sent them dollars, or when they asked for fishing tackle or seed or power saws, we sent them political advisers, or when they asked for ministers of religion, we sent them technical experts. But the point of this is not simply that we should aim to meet particular needs which those in need have identified: it is that, for a thoroughgoing solution of the problem, all the resources we have mentioned will have to be called on.

If most of these resources have not been available so far, and still are not available to the Indians and Eskimos, whose fault is it? Whether, in answering this question, we ascribe the fault to the government or to the Churches or to the electorate does not seem very important—so long as we do not pin the blame on the native peoples themselves. If we believe that government will do what most people insist it shall do, then to blame the government is really to blame the general body of citizens in relation to matters in which government has been inactive. But since the general body of citizens and the general body of Church members are still, very broadly, the same persons, we may conclude that the blame for inaction must chiefly be with those who are called Christians. This is the position adopted in this book. We shall speak of the government and of the Churches but only to make clear the immediately relevant agency. In the last analysis we are always referring to ourselves, whether as merely nominal members of the Church or as sincerely convinced members who have failed to ensure the responsibility of government. We may, however, remove at once a possible source of misunderstanding. To the extent that the Churches are bringing a moral and spiritual impact to bear on the lives of our citizens, the Churches are shaping some of the values that government, in a representative democracy, should itself represent. We are not, then, being controversial when we go on to say that in a country such as Canada, the government's job is to set an example and to help create an environment expressive of those values, so that all persons may pursue them with some reasonable prospect of success. For inevitably these values will present ends characteristic of free men; in relation to them a free government cannot simply be a bystander. It is itself committed to these ends. Wherever people seek to pursue them, the government's responsibility is to help them—if they really need help. And when Indians and Eskimos manifest a desire to escape from the stultifying conditions of their life, moving away from restraints and confinements towards greater freedom and self-direction, the government ought not to condemn them to a deeper discouragement by telling them that no one will hold them back. The question is: When these people have been so deprived and alienated, who will help them forward? A government does not necessarily or even usually show a proper respect for people's liberties by doing nothing to curtail them: its task is to help expand them.

Likewise, a responsible Church is not a "do-nothing" Church. It too must give leadership. Being occupied by the grand objectives of individual and social existence, the Church is the natural agency for formulating the purposes that liberate human life and the conditions that support that liberation. On this view of the matter, the Church among its several activities must find a place for helping people to see the ideals and the practical aspects of the ideals for which people politically should unite their strength. It can no longer be pretended that this kind of help is none of the Church's business. If it is not, whose business is it? And if, according to the tenets of the non-interventionist argument, it is no one's business, then no blame can attach to our politicians if they fail to act as if there were certain social needs and certain social groups to whose service and satisfaction the national community should be sensitive. The conclusion would not be far wrong that the non-interventionist argument has greatly restricted and partly disabled the activities of our Churches during the last century when the government itself has been zealously isolating so many of the native peoples from the main currents of our national life.

Responsibility for the neglect of our native peoples is one thing; the neglect itself is another. Because of this neglect, the gulf has continued to widen between these peoples and the immigrant settlers, so that today, despite the deeply impressive service of individual whites, the task of bridge-building between the races is in some ways more difficult than ever. But if there is one form of service for which the Churches would seem to be better equipped than any other agency, it is the building of bridges between separated persons and groups—a mission of reconciliation.

It would be true, but for most people probably misleading, to say that this mission has to be accomplished as a work of religion. If, however, "religion" is narrowly construed as that which goes on in churches or in one's own solitariness, that statement becomes largely untrue. If, for the same reason, "home missions" are so defined as to give a narrow scope to the reconciling mission, the work of religion will not be adequately done. A wider view must nowadays be taken of what religion means: equally there must be a new concept of missionary effort as traditionally understood. Were the matter otherwise, there would not be a great deal more that the Churches could attempt since already 96 per cent of all Indians and Eskimos claim membership in the Churches.[1]

In the relations between the native peoples and the whites, what must be hoped for is a growth towards partnership. In the immediate future, relations of strict partnership will be infrequent and may find their readiest expression in interracial work-camp projects within the Indian and Eskimo communities. In other instances, the whites may have to put themselves deliberately at the disposal of the native peoples and become ancillary to their plans and programmes. Even where the whites may continue for a while to relate themselves to the native peoples in a supervisory way, such a connection can no longer be paternalistic. For from now on, all groups interesting themselves in Indians and Eskimos—and especially the Churches and other religious societies—will have to operate so as to develop among these neglected fellow-citizens their full and willing and equal participation in the life and growth of Canada.

---

[1] Not all the Churches of which they are members are mentioned or dealt with in this book, since considerations of space will limit the account to those communions that have established a formal membership of at least 1 per cent of the registered Indians and Eskimos.

CHAPTER 2

The Churches and the Native Peoples

Few Christians surveying the present-day world would consider it possible to create a Christian civilization. Within Canada the same impossibility appears, even though nine out of ten of the nation's citizens claim membership in one or another of the Christian Churches. The impulses of the age are not religious. They are financial and economic. The Indians of Caughnawaga have said as much in a brief submitted in November 1965 to the federal Royal Commission on Bilingualism and Biculturalism. Their language was cruder: they spoke of our love of money. They spoke truly.

This secular spirit and ideal goes back a long way—even beyond the period of the Reformation and Counter-Reformation. The leaders of these religious movements were not leading men to a civilization that would be more firmly based on religion. The main impulse then and since has been towards a civilization based on commerce and the power of money. This impulse dominates the very beginnings of the white man's activities in Canada. The great Champlain said: "The salvation of a single soul is worth more than the conquest of an empire, and kings ought not to dream of extending their dominions into areas of idolatry except in order to bring them to submission to Jesus Christ." But there is no reason to suppose that the bringing of our native peoples to Christ was ever the prime purpose of the white man's intervention in Canada. The Merchants' Company of France, operating in Quebec, was suppressed in 1627 by Richelieu, the French Minister, for having pursued "rather their own interest than the advancement of the service of His Majesty". But there was no complaint that they had failed to put religion first. Nor, when they were replaced by the Company of One Hundred Associates, was it expected that these successors would put religion first. The priority of religion has not characterized either the history of Canada or the history of the world in the last three hundred years.

This fact has imposed severe difficulties in the way of a specifically Christian mission for the renewal of mankind—whether we are thinking of people in Canada or elsewhere, or "less-developed" or "more-developed" people. For all but a tiny minority, the sort of reason for participating in the Christian mission that was expressed by the seventeenth-century Jesuit Gabriel Lalemant seems to be born of what today—as then—is a highly unusual compound of love for God and desire for spiritual perfection. What moved him to the Canadian Indian mission field, he said, was:

> . . . my Lord and Saviour: first, to repay my debts to you; for, if *you* gave up your ease, honour, health, days and life to save *me*, a miserable creature, is it not better sense for me to use that example for giving up everything for the sake of saving those souls you regard as your very own, have loved to the death, and shed blood for?

The improbability that we can now remould the relationships of persons according to this high concept has not, however, left the Churches without some choice. The age may be overwhelmingly secular, but Christians may respond to this fact in either of two ways. They may say that Christianity is relevant only in the field of private morals and that any attempt on the part of the Churches to influence political and economic life is outside their proper jurisdiction. Alternatively, they may say that the apparent helplessness of the Churches to bring specifically Christian insights to bear on the social life of mankind increases the obligation to try to bring to bear those more general insights belonging to the common moral tradition. This tradition embodies principles not peculiar to Christianity; rather, the truths of this tradition are those that arise whenever men reflect carefully and conscientiously about their experience. These are truths that many discern but that appear to be adequately safeguarded only when Christianity becomes their defender—the need to view the person as being compact of body and soul; the need for personal liberty or freedom, and for harmonizing the liberty of the person with his security; the need to foster the family as the basic social unit; to promote unity among men irrespective of race and colour; to tame government power, to make it constitutional and an instrument of the social ends of justice.

Of these two alternative attitudes, only the latter is not self-defeating. Because it expresses certain principles of social order and political life that cannot be dismissed as Utopian, the Churches should feel able to embrace these ideas with complete seriousness and to work for them without a lurking fear that in application they must be compromised. Though they are modest aims, they carry big implications, especially at this moment for our native peoples. Freedom, justice, and security raise the question of property. Sometimes it is alleged that the Indians and Eskimos are uninterested in property, being more concerned to share than to acquire. Such an allegation forgets that what is not acquired cannot be shared. We ought not to tolerate (as at present we do) a specious form of argument that would deny to our native peoples the same property rights as we claim for ourselves. This double standard is the more despicable when we insist that private property is necessary to our own free or responsible action. What in fact we have been doing with the Indians and Eskimos—at least until a few years ago—is to withhold most property rights from them while we accumulated property to the point where there is now a grotesque inequality. We are hypocrites to talk approvingly about "those ends of personal action to which wealth is a necessary means" when, even legally, we build injustice between our races.

The great Anglican archbishop William Temple once said that Christianity was the most materialistic of all religions. He was right. He was not, of course, denying that Christianity was spiritual: the relationship that must exist between the spiritual and material is discernible through what we have called *specifically Christian* insight. But being materialistic, Christianity is concerned for a healthy body as a foundation for man's fulfilment. The Churches have a record of generous giving towards hospitals for the Indians and Eskimos, food parcels, clothing, footwear and so forth. Even since 1960, when the Diefenbaker administration produced hopes of a new deal through its Joint Parliamentary Committee on Indian Affairs, these forms of Church aid to the Indians have had to be continued. For this "charity" the Churches have been blamed in certain quarters, but what is truly to be blamed is the situation that "requires" it. Nor does the substitution of government aid for Church aid improve matters in any significant way—except to share the costs among more people. The immediately important point, however, is that the Churches cannot believe in the human being as a unity of mind and body without being concerned that this body be strong, well nourished and well cared for.

Equally, if man is this kind of unity, the Churches must be concerned for his mind. In Canada, the Churches' concern for the schooling of Indians and Eskimos has been very greatly to their credit. To the extent too that the Churches, through their schools, have fostered intellectual values, they have cared for one kind of spiritual values, preparing the way for that cleansing of insight and will that could lead a man to see the meaning of material things and his eternal destiny. Among those of our citizens, however, to whom the ultimate spiritual purpose of the Church is nonsense, it will always seem more important that the Churches should promote, among those whom they can reach, minds trained to think about affairs, to weigh evidence and bring relevant principles to bear, and so reach sound judgments that can be applied.

This point leads directly to the recognition, evident in the witness of the Churches and in the common moral tradition, that the nature of man is social and that he needs to make his concerns active through a set of social institutions. One sad consequence (there are others) of isolating our Indians on reserves has been that their social and institutional growth has been impeded for a hundred years. The Churches could and did develop the church as the highest social institution; they could and did develop the family. But on the reserves there has been a dearth of institutions for other purposes—recreation, for example. Many of the Indians knew of the institutional life of whites, and envied the whites some of these institutions; but they felt powerless, through the inertia bred by isolation, to create such institutions for themselves. Now that Indians and even Eskimos are again on the move, especially into our urban areas, an exciting challenge opens up for the Church to show respect for the social nature of these people. Likewise it presents to our Churches the opportunity to think again about the whole problem of urban adjustment, which remains unsolved even for most of the whites.

The argument in this chapter has been addressed to the Churches on behalf of a policy and programme of moderate social idealism. The great risk involved in such moderation is that, unless the Church remains aware that the base for its social operations has been made deliberately modest, it will shortly forget the compromise it made in choosing that base. In other words, there is a risk that, when the

Churches' mission is grounded in the common moral tradition, what one generation deliberately chose as a mean a later generation may carelessly reject as an extreme. Fortunately, there is a built-in check against such a risk becoming fatal: the victims of injustice will not sit quiet for ever. History will always contain its pages of reminder to the Churches that they are betraying their mission if in fact they are doing so, or—what is almost the same thing—if they are giving themselves credit for doing more to change society than in fact they are doing.

Our Indians and Eskimos have already written us a page of reminder.

CHAPTER 3

Church Missions and Church Schools

In the previous chapter, the late Archbishop Temple was quoted as saying that Christianity is the most materialistic of religions. By this he meant that Christianity cares about the bodies of men and about giving material things their proper importance. Temple was not, as we saw, thereby denying that Christianity is a spiritual religion. Nor was he affirming that the Church should not be concerned with the minds of men or with those particular spiritual values that we call the intellectual and that we associate with formal schooling. On the contrary, this kind of education—as Temple would have agreed—can help us to discern the meaning of material things and the relationship between the material and the spiritual. Nothing accidental, therefore, or merely perverse should be seen in the fact that in Canada the Church has regularly linked the provision of opportunities for religious worship with the provision of schools for the native peoples. This has been true from the earliest days of Christian missionary effort here: as early as the first half of the seventeenth century when the Jesuits carried their great mission to the Huron people, Indian youth began to be educated in schools specially established for the purpose.

As is well known, Protestant schools came later because Protestant Churches entered the Canadian mission field much later than the Roman Catholic Church. The Protestants, divided among themselves and hindered sometimes by a theology that seemed not to require a universal preaching of the gospel, eventually found themselves at work here a full century after the Recollets, Jesuits and Sulpicians. We should, however, add that, if the Anglican Church had not been weakened in the seventeenth century by the conflict in England between high churchmen and Puritans, they could have claimed title, even before the middle of that century, to a mission to North

American Indians.[1] Meanwhile, the Roman Catholic mission to the Huron "nation" had been all but destroyed in the seventeenth-century struggle of Hurons and Iroquois. Roman Catholic converts among the latter—under military pressure from the British to the south—had already in 1669 been withdrawn by the French to Caughnawaga, near Montreal. In 1732 the Moravian Brethren[2] reached North America and within twenty-five years of establishing their missions in Pennsylvania, they were up in Labrador and active among the Eskimos.[3] But for the Protestant and Roman Catholic Churches alike, the nineteenth century was the great age of missionary effort in Canada. For the Anglicans the decisive factors behind this "outreach" were, first, the Loyalist immigration from the United States after the American War of Independence[4] and, second, the Evangelical Movement which, among other things, produced the Church Missionary Society.[5] For the Roman Catholics, the decisive factor was the establishment in 1816 of a new society of missionaries—the Order of Mary Immaculate or the Oblate Order; hence, the Oblates,[6] with all the fervour of pioneers, were able to step into the gap created by the Papacy's temporary suppression of the Jesuits (1773-1814)—a suppression that delayed the re-entry of Jesuits into the Canadian mission field until 1842. Before that date, some newly established Protestant missions were being developed —by the Baptists and the Wesleyan Methodists; in 1866 the Presbyterians followed. The main Baptist mission among the Indians has always been on the Six Nations' Reserve.[7] The Baptists, then, have worked among the same group of Iroquois Indians as brought Anglican Christianity into Ontario as early as the 1780's. It was then that, out of loyalty to their long-standing political connection with the British, the Six Nations withdrew from their traditional areas in New York State following the establishment of the United States. As for the Wesleyans and Presbyterians, these—along with the Congregationalists—have formed the United Church of Canada since 1925, with a missionary outreach among the Indians (though deliberately not among the Eskimos) not unworthy of comparison with that of the Roman Catholics and Anglicans. Certain independent Presbyterian missions still survive also, and to these have latterly been added the Mennonite, Pentecostal and Baha'i missions. Nevertheless, the earliest comers to the missionary field—Roman Catholics and Anglicans—have maintained their early leads and together account for almost 80 per cent of Indian and Eskimo converts (see Appendix I). They also account for a fairly similar proportion of schools serving the educational needs of the native peoples.

The connection of missionary outreach with the setting up of these schools, Protestant and Roman Catholic alike, has been the occasion for the foregoing sketch of the growth and spread of the missionary Churches in Canada. Just as this outreach was conspicuous during the last century, so was the foundation of schools. In mentioning nineteenth-century Anglican missions we have already referred to the Evangelical Movement which was one expression of the "Second Reformation" that was permeating the Protestant Churches in Europe and bringing with it a new missionary zeal. To the Evangelical Movement we must credit the Anglican foundation of the famous Red River Valley School which, from 1820 onwards, adjoined the Roman Catholic mission at St. Boniface in what was then called Assiniboia—nowadays contained within the province of Manitoba. The Red River Settlement had been precariously established in 1811 by the Presbyterian Lord Selkirk, travelling from Hudson Bay. In 1818 the Roman Catholic Father (later Bishop) J.N. Provencher reached the Red River through Ontario. But the decisive event for Protestant schools came two years later, when the Rev. John West, an Anglican clergyman, felt moved to add to his duties (as Hudson's Bay Company[8] chaplain) the functions of principal of an inter-ethnic school. This was the aforementioned boarding school serving Indians and whites, as a result of founding which West became the first of the Evangelical missionaries to "North West America" to enjoy financial support from the Church Missionary Society. John West was in two senses a pioneer: first, because he had pastoral charge of a non-Indian agricultural settlement within a traditionally fur-bearing land which so far had excluded the very idea of agriculture; second, because in offering schooling jointly to children of Hudson's Bay Company factors and to boys and girls of Indian background, he pointed forward to a future of Indian and non-Indian equality based upon equal access to educational opportunity.

It would be easy to romanticize the Red River experiment. Though it was later paralleled or imitated by Methodist and Presbyterian "Industrial Schools" in Ontario and Saskatchewan respectively[9] and has left many marks on today's residential schools, it was an experiment full of difficulties.

In the first place, it could only hope to be a first step towards educating for those particular values we call intellectual; its primary purposes had to be moral and practical—these presented challenges enough.

The Red River school was a Christian school. Though Christianity is not essentially a system of morality, there is a morality that we think of as Christian. In any Christian education, therefore, something of this morality must be communicated; it is a morality grounded in freedom, in self-responsibility, and in the need to bear responsibility for others—not least through the functions of leadership. Books are hardly indispensable to this enterprise. But literateness, at least a minimum training of the intellectual faculties, and a capacity to read the Bible are certainly helps. The Red River school set out to provide these helps, but above all to educate the moral sense and to train for the business of leadership. It had to work with Indian students picked up at random; it had to remove these students from their native situations, isolating them in a strange environment; it had to help them catch the Rev. John West's vision of Red River as the seed-bed for a far-flung Gospel-preaching and for planting schools to serve Indians everywhere. The fact that—with some incidental failures and backslidings—Indian catechists and deacons, alumni of this school, should have been found twenty years later as far afield to the west and north as Fort Pelly, Cumberland House, and Moose Lake is remarkable.

Secondly, the school had to be practical rather than intellectual in character. Normally, a practical relevance assists the educational task, and the kind of practical programme that West's successor, Rev. William Cockran (1825), had in view implied nothing less than a practical revolution for Canada's prairies. Herein, however, lay the difficulty. To learn through "things visible and tangible" is attractive to young persons *provided that* what impinges on their five senses does not disturb their cultural prejudices. But, in Cockran's opinion, at the root of practical schooling at Red River was the recognition that settlement of the prairies by white men—when it happened, as it was already beginning to happen—would eliminate the fur economy, and the traditional way of life based upon it, and substitute agriculture and a new way of life. If, Cockran thought, the Indians

were not to suffer too terribly from the change, their training for
an agricultural life would have to begin at once.

At this point it is necessary to notice that such small-scale agriculture as had already been established among Canadian Indian groups
was regarded as "women's work", quite dishonourable for a male.
Cockran's solution was shrewd—put the boys to hog-breeding and
hog-raising and to growing the grain and potatoes to feed the hogs.
The boys would then remain in close contact with animals and with
the service of animals; yet the break with male tradition would be
profound. Put the boys to work too at raising sheep and growing
flax; with the resultant flax and wool the girls could card and spin,
weave and knit, and there would be a change in clothing traditions
comparable with that in food traditions.

It did not prove easy to change hunters into modern farming people, even in that area of Canada where this change seemed most necessary. But slowly the Indian boys at Red River managed to reconcile
themselves to what others besides Cockran were seeing as inevitable.
They were, of course, helped by the example of this fine white
teacher who shared the farm work with them. And as they came to
terms with the hoe and plough, the boys were able also to adjust
their approach to the other sex. No longer in their minds were
"women" and "dishonourable labour" linked together. This moral
by-product was matched by another: when food ceases to be merely
gathered or hunted as and when needed or most available, then the
lesson is learned that life must not be lived *in* the present chiefly
for the present, but that present effort is required to meet future
need, just as present need must be supplied from effort in the past.
The new economic way of life meant self-discipline and forethought
as well as a new form of respect for women. And the consequence
has been that from the Red River experiment in practical schooling
has stemmed today's reputation of prairie Indians as first-class
farmers and cattle-raisers.[10] In this we see an instance of the relationship of what is spiritual to what is material, of new meanings
being given to material goods, of technology affecting values.

Red River foreshadowed a whole new development in schools for
Indians. By 1829 the Wesleyan Methodists had ten day schools serving Indians in southern Ontario, with an average enrolment of
twenty-five students each. But more significant in a sense than the
multiplication of such schools were the developing ideas inspiring

their foundation. It was this which had given especial importance to the Red River experiment. (Not, of course, every aim entertained by the Rev. John West was realized; in particular his hope was frustrated that multi-tribal boarding schools would come to integrate tribe with tribe.) But it was ideas that gave especial importance to the Mount Elgin Industrial Institute—brain-child of an Indian convert, Kahkewayquonaby, more usually known as the Rev. Peter Jones. Peter Jones was from Ontario, and an able and very articulate Ojibwa chief. He had been engaged in circuit work for the Wesleyan Methodists for years when he produced a proposal to the 1844 Annual Conference of his Church, held in Brockville. He urged an experiment in Manual Labouring Schools. His idea was that boys should be instructed in farming and "useful trades", and girls in the various branches of domestic economy "so as to qualify them to be good wives and mothers". This essentially manual training would be associated with formal education of an elementary kind—reading, writing and arithmetic. There was, of course, nothing original in these ideas. But one idea *was* original.

> It is . . . our intention to select from these schools the most promising boys and girls, with a view to giving them superior advantages, so as to qualify them for missionaries and schoolteachers among their brethren. [Hence streaming of students would occur.] *No one can doubt the importance and utility of native agency in carrying forward the work of reformation.* . . . [our italics]

Peter Jones is saying that "the work of reformation" among the Indians is mainly an Indian business. No one understands Indians so well as Indians; only Indians who themselves have come to know some of the advantages of the white man's way can present to their fellows the challenge of that way with maximum effect.

> About twenty-two years ago missionaries came and preached the Gospel to us. We opened our ears to the good news. . . . Since then, several tribes have been brought into a partial state of civilization. . . . *They are anxious to participate with their white Christian friends in all those religious and civil privileges* which have made them so great. [our italics]

And then comes the statement so apparently discordant with the ideal of family unity yet so necessary to the beginning of any "work of reformation" among the simpler peoples[11] through the educational process:

Indian parents have repeatedly said to me that they would *gladly con-sign [their children] over to the care of suitable teachers for a certain number of years*, that they might learn the arts of civilized life.[12] [our italics]

There is no reason to suppose that these statements were make-believe. On the contrary, they must have been a reliable report of Indian public opinion in southern Ontario in the matter both of Indian interest in "the arts of civilized life" and the willingness of Indians to send their children away from home to learn these arts. Otherwise, the Indians at Muncey would not have given two hundred acres for the school buildings and farm at Mount Elgin, or contributed generously towards the costs of erection. This project was clearly something to which the Indians themselves attached high priority, and the principles and purposes underlying the project are those that would be welcome at the present day.

Did the Mount Elgin Industrial Institute fulfil the original expectations? Probably every educational enterprise, founded in high hope, disappoints that hope. But we are told that by the third generation, "many are employed in factories and flaxmills", some in engineering and railroad occupations, one or two in school teaching, most on farms or in their homes, while Mount Elgin alumni from several different Protestant persuasions are playing a full part in the Church.

But perhaps more significant than the variety of "civilized arts" represented by the vocational achievements of these alumni was that, at this period, before the Age of the Treaties removed the Indian population into literally thousands of reserves, there appeared to exist a spontaneous Indian demand to be taken into partnership by the whites. If Peter Jones is to be believed, the Indians—or many of them—were interested in sharing with whites the goals of modern "religious and civil" society. They were disposed to learn from non-Indians and to communicate to fellow Indians the "arts of civilized life", not least to give freely for the "work of reformation" among their own people, lending "native agency" to purposes they could understand and hence could identify themselves with.

Another significance in the Mount Elgin experiment should also be noticed. Not only did Peter Jones stress the importance of "native agency"—a point that it has taken us more than one hundred years to give sufficient importance to—but he also stressed, as the passage already quoted makes clear, the need for "streaming" Indian students at school, selecting "the most promising", giving them "superior advantages" so that they might have the intellectual equipment and training for leadership. This is perhaps where the schools have encountered their greatest difficulties and their greatest need for linking their slender resources to the much greater resources, financial and human, available through the State. Intellectual training has turned out to be an expensive business. And this explains why the State has found itself compelled to enter, and more recently to control, the whole field of education. The residential schools which the Churches pioneered are now State-supported and almost entirely State-owned, though still administered by the Churches. To the sixty-six residential schools[13] are now added 363 federal Indian day schools and 1,075 non-Indian schools serving Indians. There are, of course, other schools, day and residential, now serving Eskimos. But perhaps more indicative of the movement of events is the fact that, whereas only a few hundred boys and girls from among our native peoples were at school a century ago, today almost sixty thousand are at school, a higher percentage are completing high school, and a few are reaching university.

These developments—statistically outlined in Chapter 6—raise important questions for the Churches: when such large-scale consequences have sprung from such small beginnings, how valuable in the Church's view are these consequences? How well are these purposes being served by arrangements under which the Churches, as pioneers of schools for the native peoples, are either replaced by the State as providers of schools or, in effect, operate as agents on behalf of the State? Granted that one purpose of a school system is to transmit a cultural heritage from one generation to the next and that, as Canadians, we are, and ought to be, engaged in trying to build a truly integrated society, ought not our teaching to take into account the cultural diversity of Canada and, consistently with proper respect for the political aim of integration and national unity, ought not this teaching to show respect for the cultural sensibilities of the native peoples?

To these questions we shall return in Chapter 7. Before then we shall outline the story, from the mid-nineteenth century onwards, of developments among the native peoples and of Christian missionary outreach to them.

1 The Puritan apostolate of the Rev. John Eliot (1604-1690) went unrecognized at first by the Church of Archbishop Laud. Eliot had emigrated from England to Massachusetts in 1631—"for conscience' sake". Like the Jesuits before him, he had taken pains to master the local Indian language before starting his mission (1646). In 1649, he managed to inspire, back in England, the setting-up of a corporation "for the promoting and propagating of the gospel among the Indians of New England". Eliot's converts, and those of other ministers who joined him later, were said to have numbered 3,700, in and outside Massachusetts, by the time the tragic war with the Indian King Philip broke out in 1675. The war brought a rapid decline in the first successful, large-scale Protestant mission to the North American Indians—a decline not arrested until the eighteenth century.

2 Otherwise known as "Unitas Fratrum". These latter-day followers of John Hus of Moravia had been reorganized in 1722 by the German Protestant leader, Count von Zinzendorf.

3 See also Chapter 4.
Some of the most celebrated Loyalist immigrants were members of the famous Iroquoian Indian Confederacy which, by the eighteenth century, came to be known as "The Six Nations". The great majority of these people were converted by the Anglicans; from the days of Queen Anne (1702-14), they have deeply cherished this connection, and since the 1780's they have preserved it both at Deseronto, Ontario (Mohawks of Tyendinaga on the Bay of Quinte), and near Brantford, Ontario (Six Nations of the Grand River). A minority of the Six Nations, however, have clung to their traditional Long House religion which is said to have been quite strongly influenced by Quakerism as mediated through an eighteenth-century Indian called Handsome Lake.

5 The C.M.S., founded in 1799, was an outcome of the Evangelical Revival in eighteenth-century England. Among its earliest supporters were a few zealous Anglicans (among whom William Wilberforce was included) who are known to history as the "Clapham Sect". The name was given to this group because they lived at Clapham near London, worshipping in the parish church under John Venn as vicar. It is worth noting at this stage that when the C.M.S. and the Hudson's Bay Company shared in supporting a missionary-chaplain at the Red River Settlement in 1820, the Governors of the Company numbered earnest evangelicals among its members. It is also worth pointing out (a) that the C.M.S. provided the second thrust to Anglican missions to North America (the first having been the Society for the Propagation of the Gospel in 1701), (b) that the termination by the C.M.S. of its mission work in Canada in 1920 has proved a severe check.

6 "Oblates" means, literally, those offered (to God). Though it is not a term exclusive to members of this Order, it has become attached in popular use to this Order.

7 There had been a number of Baptist adherents since about 1835, as a consequence of the missionary labours of two ministers from New York State; the first church was built in 1840.

8 In 1670 King Charles II of England granted charter to his cousin Prince Rupert

and to seventeen other shareholders to form the Hudson's Bay Company, and to this company he gave not only all subordinate powers of lordship and government but the sole right to trade in "Rupert's Land", i.e. within that vast region stretching from Northern Quebec to the Rockies and northwards towards the Barren Lands, which was watered by rivers flowing to the Bay. In the 1780's the H.B.C., based in London (England), met a furious competitor, and interloper within its own territories, in the shape of the North West Fur Company based in Montreal. The few score officers or factors of the H.B.C.— confined until the later eighteenth century to "factories" located on the Bay —were hardly able to enforce against the interloping Fur Company from Montreal the rights that were legally theirs. The charter might prescribe that no one—Indian or other—could trade furs or other goods except with and through the Company; but this did nothing to stop the North West Fur Company from penetrating Rupert's Land as far west as the Rockies, setting up their posts, doing deals with the Indians and filching much of the trade. This inter-company struggle was not only ruinous to the companies until it was ended in 1821 (when the North West Company agreed to amalgamate with its rival and take its name); it was ruinous also to very many Indians who found themselves taking the brunt of this ruthless rivalry, suffering moral and physical hurt as the competitors poured out rum and brandy for the Indians in the attempt to win or keep their loyalty, service and patronage. The North West Company, being a loose commercial partnership (unlike its competitor), was scarcely able to attempt any control over the behaviour of its officers towards Indian women. As a consequence, by 1820 the Company found itself burdened with between 1,200 and 1,500 individuals—Indian and Métis (or half-breed) women and their children. Though not all of these officers neglected their consorts and offspring and though some of them were entirely faithful to their Indian wives, the picture presented by this long episode is dark. The Anglican and Roman Catholic missions into Assiniboia helped bring this episode to a close.

[9] The Wesleyan Methodists' Mount Elgin Industrial School at Muncey, Ontario (founded 1849), and the Presbyterians' Industrial School at Regina, Saskatchewan (founded 1890).

[10] For example, in a publication issued in 1915, the Presbyterian Women's Missionary Society reported that "Some of the best farmers in the File Hills Colony are from Regina" where, with government financing, the Presbyterian Church had operated an Industrial School for twenty years, up to 1910.

[11] Contemporary authors on social affairs have tortured themselves trying to find adjectives that describe the simpler peoples without seeming to insult them. Hence come such expressions as "less developed" or "developing" or "less complex". I hope no reader will stick at the use of the word "simpler": if we were morally simpler, we would be more developed.

[12] *The Missionary Bulletin*, Vol. XVI, No. 2 (Toronto: Missionary Society of the Methodist Church), pp. 161-208.

[13] Some of these function simply as hostels. Six of the residential schools are fully owned by the Churches.

CHAPTER 4

Changing Perspective in Mission

In a short book such as this, there is no space to tell the complete story of Christian missions in Canada, even during the last century. But such a story would be one of missionary thrusts into the West and northwards into the Arctic along the Atlantic and Pacific as well as through the forests, lakelands, and Barren Lands between Alaska and Hudson Bay. Even those people who believe the missionary enterprise to be completely mischievous would have to admire the Christian men who, a century ago, were sacrificing comfort and ease, ignoring danger, forever taking a difficult initiative, and performing prodigies of labour in arduous climates and desolate wastes. As for the men who dedicated themselves to this enterprise believing it to be the most important work on earth, they must sometimes have wryly pondered, as did an Oblate Father[1]: "Truly, God must dearly love each one of his children to draw me so far to serve so few."

Many thousands of Indians and Eskimos were reached, nevertheless, by this missionary zeal. Though the story cannot be told, it must at least be illustrated. Since we shall illustrate it chiefly from the work of three men—William Duncan, William Carpenter Bompas and E. J. Peck—of the Anglican Church, we shall more easily escape the charge of arbitrary selection if we start by mentioning the tremendous impetus given to Roman Catholic missions in our country by the Papacy's recognition in 1826 of the Oblate Order—the Order of Mary Immaculate.[2] It had been founded ten years earlier by a former member of the French professional nobility, Eugène de Mazenod (later, Bishop of Marseilles). To pay tribute to this Order and its most distinguished missionaries in Canada is not to overlook the outstanding contributions made through other Roman Catholic Orders.[3] But it is to indicate that the Oblates, from the beginning, have felt a deep sense of pity for those in material wretchedness. This pity is revealed in the actual scriptural motto of the Order: "He sent me to bring the good news to *poor* people."[4] With the Oblates, the pity is no longer restricted or even directed to "heathen blindness in bowing down to wood and stone". By distinction the Oblates have shown themselves to be sensitively aware of the cultural foundation upon which the religious and educational effort of their Order can be built. But, principally, while discouraging among their converts any "desire after wealth . . . tinctured with luxury", they have positively encouraged a constructive approach to the social problems of material deprivation characterizing almost the entire native population of Canada until recently. It is this that constitutes the new emphasis of their work.[5]

It is this too that is reminiscent of the work of the first of our selected Anglican missionaries, William Duncan of British Columbia—admittedly a controversial figure in the history of his Church but a man to whom even his enemies must have conceded an immense productivity. His manifold services to West Coast Indians included being "lay pastor and missionary, treasurer . . . clerk of works, head master, counsellor in general . . . [and] a magistrate [dispensing] justice . . . along the whole coast."[6] Through him, the evangelization of the British Columbia coastal tribes was carried northward from Fort Simpson. But more distinctive was his attempt to establish a "Christian Indian and model settlement" at Metlakahtla; it showed in paternalistic form many external features of the contemporary movement of "community development", though community development and paternalism are in essence contradictory. Whatever judgment we may offer on Duncan's later career when in 1887 he and nine hundred Indians emigrated to southern Alaska, his work among almost all of the Indians whose lives he touched seems to have had permanently creative effects.

William Carpenter Bompas, who became a bishop, was a more orthodox type of missionary, winning souls for the Church and extending its administration. A man of simple faith and good humour, he travelled along the great lakes and rivers, down to the Arctic Ocean and over the Rocky Mountains, meeting Indians and Eskimos in their tents and igloos, setting up mission stations and building the Church. Dividing and subdividing his original diocese, he left behind him three bishoprics: Selkirk (now the Yukon), Athabaska and Mackenzie. With the aid of the men he introduced to northern missions and through their immediate successors, Arctic mission stations came into being among the Loucheux Indians on the Porcupine River, on Coronation Gulf, and on Herschel Island.

Peck's mission belonged to the eastern Arctic. Originally at Great Whale River[7] (a mixed Indian-Eskimo area), the Reverend E. J. Peck was seized with the ambition of extending his mission to Ungava Bay on the opposite coastline of northern Quebec. Trying four times in three years, Peck managed at last to reach Fort Chimo, though in circumstances that required his return after a stay of only three weeks. But the three-week mission had permanent effects: a converted Eskimo (perhaps there was more than one) himself decided to go further north still—across Hudson Strait to Baffin Island. Encouraged by this, Peck removed himself in 1894 lock, stock and barrel to Blacklead Island in Cumberland Sound. From there he carried out the work of ministry, schooling the young and educating adults with a degree of success that ensured the spread of missions to Lake Harbour, Pangnirtung and other points in the High Arctic.

These three short sketches provide hints of a fascinating missionary record which can be studied in available books,[8] published denominationally. But a few more broad strokes are necessary to convert these hints into clues to the whole record. We have already indicated that the direction of missionary advance was first of all from the East into the West. There the names of the distinguished Wesleyan missionary and inventor of Cree syllabics, James Evans (Norway House and westward) and the equally distinguished Roman Catholic Father Albert Lacombe (Alberta) have great importance in the middle half of the nineteenth century. The lines of advance then turned northward. The Oblate Fathers, for example, worked northward from the prairies, and their landmarks and milestones are Ile-à-la-Crosse and Caribou Lake in 1846-48 (Father, later Archbishop, Taché); Lake Athabaska and Great Slave Lake in 1847-50 (Father, later Bishop, Faraud); and the lower Mackenzie and Peel River in 1860, where the first contacts with the Eskimos occurred (Father Grollier). Likewise in British Columbia, where the establishment of some very tenacious and (in Christian eyes) very unlovely forms of paganism compounded the missionary's problems, the Roman Catholics were able to achieve a greater success than any other communion. At the same time, what we now call the

United Church obtained in British Columbia more converts than it had done in any other province, not excluding Ontario where its Methodist component had for so long been active. In particular, medical missions were an important part of the United Church's work in the islands and on the coast, and these—together with the religious groups spread along the Pacific—were developed and held together by boat. Among thousands of British Columbia Indians, Captain Oliver of the launch *Thomas Crosby* became a household name, as he brought doctors, preachers and teachers on their circuits or to their stations. This development was not unlike another which was taking place along the upper Atlantic coastline, where, from 1892 onwards, the Anglican medical doctor (later Sir) Wilfred Grenfell was building up hospitals, nursing stations and co-operative groups in desolate Labrador, developing "the Grenfell Mission" on a strictly non-denominational basis and opening it to persons of every race, colour and creed.[9]

In the opening paragraph of this chapter we mentioned—though it was scarcely necessary—that the missionary enterprise is nowadays a most controversial subject. As far back as the early eighteenth century, we find a broadside against missions in Matthew Green's poem "The Spleen":

> *When gospel propagators say,*
> *We're bound our great light to display,*
> *And Indian darkness drive away. . . .*
> *This view my forward zeal so shocks,*
> *In vain they hold the money-box.*

It is true that Green makes the poor calibre of missionaries the basis of his charge. At the same time, he also makes clear that a certain presumption of superiority on the part of the missionary and the risks entailed in shattering other (and simpler) people's cultural ideas and ways are further disturbing features of Christian missions. How can these doubts and objections be answered?

First, no true missionary will consider himself superior to those among whom he has to work. Second, he will avoid shattering the ideas and ways of these people. He would not, of course, be a missionary if he did not suppose he had something to teach them and some good news to bring them. How difficult it is to suppose this while keeping humble and ready to learn from others in return is a matter of observation—and not only on the mission field. It is equally difficult to avoid creating the impression that "the new thing" which it is the missionary's job to introduce must destroy the old rather than fulfil it. Yet these difficulties do not invalidate the missionary enterprise. They suggest it must be carried out with skill as well as commitment, with a sense for the truth in other people as well as for their well-being and happiness, and above all with genuine friendliness.

There are three implications of these remarks.

A Christian missionary is not someone who, in his essential character and responsibility, is different from any other Christian, lay or ordained. He is our paid delegate. But if our own physical situation and if our own domestic or professional commitments were other than they are, we might well be doing his job in his place, with precisely the same expectations pressing upon us.

Next, whatever springs out of a direct Christian relationship with another human being is, according to this view, a sort of missionary activity. The basis of it will always be religious—a responding to a spiritual prompting within ourselves, an answering of the same spirit within others; but its form and appearance may be anything at all, from the simple friendship of social intercourse to caring for the body in a hospital, for the mind in a school, and for the soul in worship. There are no arbitrary limits on the occasions and content of Christian relationship.

Third, a Christian relationship will always be an equal relationship from which each partner will hope to receive at least as much as he may be called upon to try to give.[10] It will, of course, be a relationship "in love", and hence there will be that sensitivity to the feelings and declared needs of the other persons that we expect in this kind of relationship.

At this point we may perhaps discern one very serious danger in traditional missionary activity. If it is construed as specifically *evangelistic*—the carrying of certain religious beliefs and practices to other people who are considered to be spiritually blind or in grievous error—then the evangelist looks only to a notional acceptance by these other people of what he serves as the bearer. Such a notional acceptance may bring no kind of spiritual gift in return but be a mere statistic for the records—a conversion born of self-interest or transacted like a double insurance policy, as the Vietnamese have produced their "rice Christians" and the Kikuyu of Kenya their "book Christians". Such a conversion has no staying power. If trial and tribulation come along and prudential reasons no longer operate in favour of the claim to Christian faith and performance, there can be a definite return to the original paganism—as has not infrequently occurred in Canada. Describing the situation in a prairie reserve in August 1918, one writer had this to say:

> ... conditions were awfully discouraging. There we have had an example of independent, self-sacrificing devotion to the cause of Christianity which cannot be excelled elsewhere. A. F.'s character and work have been of the very best. Years and years of comparative neglect by the Church had caused discouragement and despair to come. . . . Now . . ., under a great fear, they had made a relapse into pagan practices.[11] A. had become discouraged and had given up his work. . . . Then they turned against me. Threats had been made on my life if I came. There was no welcome for me. There was a feeling colder than Greenland.[12]

Experiences of this sort reinforce the need to be clear about the proper nature of missionary activity. Reappraisal of Christian missions is rather a feature of the present century, and distinguished opinion might be quoted. But the following words were written by a Canadian who was a Methodist (later, a United Church) missionary among the Indian people, and we prefer to quote him, disjointed though his words are, because they reflect with patent sincerity the movement of ideas in the mind of a man trying to grapple with the question of what his role ought to be. The writer was Roy C. Taylor, from the Battle River Indian Mission at Ponoka, Alberta, and he was addressing fellow missionaries whom he was rejoining after an absence resulting from service overseas in World War I:

> Coming back to this work . . ., it might be of interest to my brethren for me to venture a few remarks as to the present status of the Indian, materially and spiritually, as gleaned from a reconnaissance of the work on this particular mission. . . .
>
> In a material sense, I make bold to say that there has been some little progress. . . . [The] people are seeing the advantages of the farmer's life and are forsaking the nomadic life for a more stable means of support. To encourage and vitalize this slumbering ambition is a task worthy of your very best efforts. It is perfectly obvious why this is so. A system

which has created a great family of wards, dependent on the Government for direction and very largely for subsistence, must inevitably kill personal incentive. . . .

A word or two with reference to the spiritual status of the Indian: it would appear that in this he has been pauperized. Much devoted Christian work has been done and is being done, but somehow we must confess that here, as well as in the material life, we have missed the mark. . . .

Hitherto, it would appear that the missionary, *from the Indians' standpoint*, has been useful in so far as he ministered to their bodily needs. Spiritually he has been little in demand, as evidenced by the sparsely occupied pews in our churches as compared with the packed dance halls and crowded pow-wows. . . .

A great spiritual awakening will follow in the wake of a keen community spirit, by which the greatest good to the greatest number is engendered.[13]

This letter tumbles forth the impressions which the old scene freshly produces on the returned missionary's more experienced eye. In that particular area of Alberta, the Indians are seeing the advantages of a settled agricultural life; as a result, there has been a small economic improvement. But Indian ambition "slumbers"; "personal incentive" is killed; the government has created "a great family of wards". The Church too has "missed the mark". Only in what pertains to the "material" side of the Indian's life is the Church greatly valued. Spiritually the Church "has been little in demand"—witness the many empty pews; socially, it has been neglected for the crowded dance halls and pow-wows.

Why? Because the Indian has been left without the *need* to set new goals for his common social life; hence, he appears to lack the *will* and the *morale* to create these goals for the greatest good of the greatest number.

And the solution? The "great awakening" will come when somehow a "keen community spirit" can be generated.

Roy Taylor is saying, in effect, that the Church's most central, spiritual task will be achieved when, and only when, Christian missions can be made to relate to the real situation of people and, most important of all, to their need—however hidden or dormant—to build together a meaningful community life. In effect too, Roy Taylor is providing a new and wider definition of the Christian missionary. It is no accident that Roy Taylor mentions first the economic life of the Indians; then passes to their psychological state;

and concludes with references to their social and religious or spiritual condition. In a manner perhaps a little obscure even to himself, he is propounding the idea that missions work to secure the *total well-being* of our native peoples, their spiritual health being included therein.

---

[1] I am quoting from memory and perhaps slightly inaccurately: I have been unable to check the source of the quotation.

[2] See also Chapter 3.

[3] In particular, the names of the Jesuits St. Jean de Brébeuf (d. 1649) and St. Isaac Jogues (d. 1646) should be remembered.

[4] This concern for those suffering an excessive poverty links the Oblates with the Quakers who, while they never developed a mission to the native peoples of Canada, did establish in 1845 a "Negroes and Aborigines Fund". Though used primarily for U.S. peoples, it also helped many distressed Canadian Indians.

[5] The Oblates have worked primarily through the agency of schools. In 1958, of the forty-four residential schools under Roman Catholic auspices, forty-one were administered by the Oblates. Three-quarters of these were in the West.

[6] Canon S. Gould, former General Secretary of the Anglican Missionary Society of the Canadian Church (M.S.C.C.).

[7] Great Whale River has been developed from the Anglican base in the bishopric of Moosonee.

A neglected fact of missionary history is that one Church often helps another even if this is not intended. For example, John Horden, the first Bishop of Moosonee, would not have made such immediate progress at Moose Factory (1851) without the ground having been prepared by the Methodists. Nor, without the help of an Eskimo interpreter who had been converted by Moravian missionaries in Labrador, would Bishop Horden have been so successful in carrying his work northwards to Great Whale River.

[8] How tantalizing and inadequate these hints are is evidenced by some remarks made by Dr. J. R. Millman, General Synod Archivist for the Anglican Church of Canada, who very kindly read this book in manuscript and made several important suggestions for its improvement. He urged that no book claiming to deal with the relationships of the Churches of Canada with the native peoples should fail to mention the following two nineteenth-century churchmen: the Rev. Edward F. Wilson and the Rev. Silas Tertius Rand. The latter had the Maritimes as his base, translating hymns, the scriptures, catechisms and prayer books into ten native languages (excluding several dialects of Cree). The former founded the Shingwauk and Wawanosh Schools in Sault Ste Marie, and edited *Our Forest Children* and *The Canadian Indian*. It is Dr. Millman's opinion that "for thirty years" (he died in 1915) "no individual in Canada toiled more devotedly for the Indian than Edward Wilson—yet today he is a forgotten man."

[9] In his Report to the Directors in 1916, Dr. Grenfell said: "We have members

of practically every Christian denomination among us—Episcopalians, Congregationalists, Presbyterians, Methodists, Unitarians, and Roman Catholics . . . To the best of our ability, in the ways we know best, and think most advisable, we agree to try and spread the knowledge of Christ . . . [But] proselytizing will not be permitted among our fraternity."

10 Compare the remarks of two Quakers: first of George Fox, the founder of Quakerism: "Let your light shine among the Indians . . . *that ye may answer the truth in them.*" Second, of John Woolman: ". . . thence arose a concern to spend some time with the Indians, that I might feel and understand the spirit they live in, *if haply I might receive some instruction from them, or they might be in any degree helped forward by my following the leadings of truth among them.*" [Italics ours.]

11 Mr. W. I. C. Wuttunee, leader of the National Indian Council of Canada, addressing the Board of Evangelism and Social Service of the United Church at its annual meeting in Toronto in 1964, objected strongly to the use of the word "pagan" in connection with the Indian religions. But "pagan" is certainly correct usage.

12 *The Missionary Bulletin*, Vol. XVI, No. 2 (Toronto: Missionary Society of the Methodist Church), p. 221

13 *Ibid.*, pp. 223-6.

CHAPTER 5

Some Historical Roots of Today's Problems

The United Church missionary Roy Taylor has just been quoted as saying that the system under which the Indians of Canada have come to live has "killed incentive", transforming them into "a great family of wards, dependent on the government for direction and very largely for subsistence". These are strong words. But, though their truth has been somewhat qualified[1] since the Indian Act of 1951, the system remains very largely intact, and Taylor's description of its effects by the time of its full development is quite accurate. His words were written in 1920; for the origins of the system we must go back a half century and even longer.

Throughout that earlier period, a fairly close correspondence had existed between the white Canadian attitude to the native peoples and the official policy towards them, though the latter had usually been rather ahead of public opinion. Since this opinion was at best indifferent, and since in any case these peoples, or at least the Indians who were administered by the Indian Affairs Branch,[2] have been excluded until recently from even a small voice in the larger policy controlling them, our interpretation of that policy and of developments in it will essentially be an account of the relations established by the government with the native people.

In the matter of native affairs, Ottawa has, of course, been heir of the British crown. We might also add that Ottawa is heir too of the Hudson's Bay Company which, because of certain exclusive rights it enjoyed in regions watered by rivers flowing to Hudson Bay, had come quite early to have a special connection with western and northern Indians and also the Eskimos. The subsequent affairs of Eskimos, however, have not been dealt with in the same way as those of Indians. Legally, Ottawa does not distinguish Eskimos as she distinguishes Indians from other Canadians, and one aspect of

33

this is that Eskimos—except where (as in the Arctic) provincial governments do not exist—have not been brought under special federal jurisdiction.[3] By contrast, under the British North America Act of 1867, the provincial governments were excluded from responsibility for "Indians and Indian lands". Consistently with this, the Hudson's Bay Company, when it surrendered in 1870 its exclusive rights throughout the regions watered by rivers flowing to the Bay, found that such of its governmental functions as would thereafter attach to provincial jurisdiction were entrusted to the government of the new province of Manitoba while within the federal government itself were vested its responsibilities towards the native peoples.[4]

As heir of the imperial tradition, the Government of Canada has, in part, sustained that tradition and, in part, broken with it—as may be seen from a brief review of the Canadian government's trusteeship or wardship during the period ending with the codifying of the Indian Act of 1951. One aspect of that tradition had been its diffidence about imposing its own particular ideas and way of life upon those of different cultural heritage. Accordingly, the federal government has itself avoided exercising over the native peoples a positive form of "wardship" or guardianship. Paternalism, however, it has not avoided—a negative paternalism or regulatory protection and restraint, from which was absent for too long almost all challenges to consider new values and to seize new opportunities consistent with them. This not unkindly paternalistic *laissez-faire* has proved a failure. Since World War II, the government has been aware of this and, while anxious to find the way towards a new approach, has shown itself defensive about the old one. Hence, until the last year or two when a more self-confident, positive and relaxed attitude has become apparent, Ottawa—not implausibly—has been advertising the anthropological insight that what people themselves see to be their needs and themselves desire to do to meet them has much more importance than what others infer to be those needs and undertake to supply.

Another feature of the imperial tradition had been its respect for the land-base needs of the indigenous peoples—a respect that, in the eighteenth century, had brought Westminster up against white opposition in the Thirteen Colonies. Even before Britain transferred to Canada in 1860 its responsibilities for "Indians and Indian lands", it had been under pressure from white settlers and immigrants to modify its policies *vis à vis* the native inhabitants. It is safe to say, however, that the Imperial Parliament would not have been so sensitive to white Canadian pressures as was the new Canadian Parliament, even though by 1867 the needs of two and a half million whites were irresistible in comparison with those of under two hundred thousand Indians. Changes in the direction of economic occupation of land by whites would have come more slowly or less drastically, or they would have been compassed in a manner less damaging to Indian interests than those imposed through the Government of Canada. But as soon as the management of Indian affairs fell into the hands of the Crown Lands Department of the Province of Canada, the great movement began for the transaction of public "Treaties" with the Indian groups.[5] Those of 1860 and 1862, covering areas along or within Lake Huron or Superior, set the pattern for those following Confederation, from 1871 onwards. Eleven numbered Treaties and two unnumbered ones have since come into being, rendering enormous tracts of land "available for settlement" by whites, and setting aside a large number of relatively tiny reserves "for the use and benefit of Indians". It would be a mistake to assume that all the Indians entered freely into Treaty. Usually the initiative lay with the Canadian government. Often the Treaties were negotiated with much hard bargaining and considerable Indian dissatisfaction. Most significantly, only about half of the Indian population has yet consented to Treaty relations. "Outside Treaty" still are the Indians of British Columbia (except in the northeastern tip), the Indians of Quebec, New Brunswick, Nova Scotia, Prince Edward Island and mainland Newfoundland, together with sundry immigrant Indian groups (Sioux as well as Iroquois) in Manitoba and Ontario. Nevertheless, the placing of Indians on reserves has proceeded apace wherever it was necessary to make land "available for settlement", irrespective of whether Treaties were being concluded. And it is this process that constituted the largest innovation between the surrender of control by the Imperial Parliament and the passing of the Indian Act in 1951. The isolation of the Indians within their 558 bands spread over 2,200 reserves, out of sight and largely out of mind of most white Canadians, has been a "protective" act whose consequences form the major part of the Indian problem in the current era.

"Reserve-dwelling" in the last one hundred years has brought a peculiar status as well as a new way of life for Indians. One feature of this status, until the Diefenbaker administration modified it by conferring the federal voting right upon Indians, was their disfranchisement.[6] (Even today, there are provinces in Canada where Indians may not vote in provincial elections.) Another and more important feature is the linking of this legal status with property interests and with "normal residence on a reserve". The nature of these interests as they relate to land and their implications as they relate to free contract, security for credit, and the raising of capital from non-Indian sources, have proved far-reaching and have posed questions for which no adequate answers have yet been supplied. If the status of an Indian exempts him, on action by a non-Indian, from pledge, mortgage, seizure and distraint of such property-interests as were not acquired under conditional sales agreements, he is unlikely to be able to procure necessary credit from ordinary sources for productive enterprise. Hence, present Indian status is an obstacle to security for those loans which chartered banks might be willing to extend if Indian status were differently construed. To an economist it would be plain that the right of property is basic to all other real rights, since it is the necessary pre-condition of exchange. But an Indian has no right of ownership of the land he may possess and occupy in a reserve. He is caught up in a pre-modern system of property relations which hinders exchange, the transfer of the means of production, and the division of labour, and all too often he utterly lacks the incentives to "call forth the exertions necessary for supplying the means of expenditure". Hence, his reserves have become enclaves of acute poverty, largely deficient in economic enterprise, where the skill—as one observer has put it—of obtaining social assistance must equal the skill of hunting and trapping.

We cannot claim that this disability of the Indian's legal status—the obverse of his doubtful privileges—has passed unnoticed or underrated. One West Coast Indian band council has suggested that the "protection" of Indian property be abolished in respect of bands deemed by the government to be "advanced". Though the government has not so far acted on this, it has adopted a variant, and arrangements have been introduced whereby a revenue-receiving band council will underwrite a loan from a non-Indian to one (or even a group) of its band members, on condition that the collateral property interest is pledged to itself. So long as Indian legal status remains, further ingenuity in this particular direction is required, for present devices—though not useless—are minimal in their effect.[7] Band councils deemed to be "advanced" may raise money and even control the revenue (but not the capital) section of their shares, in the Indian Trust Funds held in Ottawa. But the pace of "advancement" has been so slow that by 1965 only ninety-two band councils (or about 18 per cent) were free, under Section 68, subsection 1, of the Indian Act, to manage their trust fund shares. It is therefore clear that credit, as a particular mode of production enabling more wealth to be produced, is urgently needed and that it must largely come from government sources. The Revolving Loan Fund for Indians, now fixed at one million dollars to serve the needs of over two hundred thousand people, is hopelessly inadequate. Yet so long as Indians remain outside the mainstream of Canadian life and permeated by under-development and demoralization, private sources of credit to Indians (except for consumption, where it is least desirable) will continue to be merely marginal.

If the government now sees that the first priority in Indian affairs is to combat poverty and to build up economic opportunity, it also recognizes that a number of factors have come into prominence since Confederation which render the situation very awkward.

First, since reserves were created primarily in order to render certain areas available for settlement by whites, no reserves were created in areas where the whites had ample opportunities for any settlement in which they might be interested. Hence, no reserves were anywhere created for Eskimos in the Northland; none were created for the Indians in Labrador or in the far-flung Northwest Territories. While some problems affect all the native peoples wherever they live, other problems are peculiar to the reserve-dwelling Indians and appear less tractable than the former.

Second, the administrative inconveniences now attending the provision of services to Indian reserves can hardly be annulled by a stroke of the pen when memory is still green that the Government created the reserves partly for its own administrative convenience. When the Indians become so habituated to the custodial care imposed upon them that they attach more importance to the minimal security conferred by their status than to the disability of their dependence, then the Government finds itself in a position where it cannot unscramble, without the suggestion of treachery, what it has scrambled.

Third, too many of the reserves have become centres of shiftlessness and inertia. The under-development of reserves is depressing each new generation of children. Where with unusual energy of mind some Indians have broken free of the reserve system or, through historical accident have, like the Eskimos and Métis, never known it, they have retained or regained a measure of self-respect which hopefully will ensure that, as government aid to them becomes more adequate, they will respond to it and use it as (according to theory) free men should. But how to secure a similar response from the reserve-dwellers is still an unsolved problem.

We have said that where no settlement problems occurred for the whites, no reserves were set up for those legally defined and "registered" as Indians. But in addition to registered Indians there are, as we have noted, many persons of Indian background and heritage (called Métis) who are not "registered Indians".[8] Although they may be living therefore as neighbours or intermarrying with reserve-dwelling, registered Indians, no reserves have anywhere been set aside for *them* (since their forebears took a cash settlement instead). To complicate matters further: although certain Eskimos were, on one occasion, deemed by a court of law to be Indians in the meaning of the B.N.A. Act,[9] they have never been granted reserves, are not disfranchised, and have only been given "registration" (by the device of number-discs) to ensure their individual identification by officers of government. These legal and constitutional peculiarities have made impossible a uniform policy towards the native peoples. The Métis and those few Eskimos who are living within *provincial* areas may now be assisted in their development through provisions in the Agricultural Rehabilitation and Development Act of 1961 (ARDA). For that larger number of Eskimos who live in the Northwest Territories or the Yukon Territory, government assistance is given through a variety of federal agencies whose work is co-ordinated and sometimes discharged by the Northern Administration Branch. The operations of the federal government may occur either directly or indirectly through the territorial governments, and in the field of schooling and higher education the Northern Administration Branch has been acting both on behalf of the white population and as agent of the Indian Affairs Branch. To complete this account of the administrative machinery, we need only add that Indians living in provinces may be served directly by the Indian Affairs Branch or by the provincial governments acting for the Branch.

This account of the changes of the last one hundred years, which have now brought the bulk of the Indian people into the situation just described, has been primarily linked to changes in the Indian land base. But the most important of the meanings that attach to these territorial changes concern the attitudes of those who caused them and of those who suffered them.

Those who caused them were the whites, for they were interested in removing Indians to particular areas where they would not interfere with their own economic projects. Hence, as we have seen, reserves were set aside for the Indians and, wherever feasible, the transaction of so-called Treaties accompanied the establishment of these reserves. It is fashionable nowadays to claim that the reserves and the Treaties were for the more adequate protection of Indians— in other words, to safeguard them from the exploitation of unscrupulous whites. In every major transaction affecting the fortunes of a whole people, we would be surprised if some variety were not to be found in the underlying motives. In the present instance we cannot deny that, when certain Treaties were arranged, a protective, custodial regard for Indian well-being was an element in the minds of Crown officers. Two points, however, are extremely pertinent. First, the protection of Indians from what the nineteenth-century missionary, Father Constantine Scollen, has called "the abominable traffic of whisky" no more depended on Treaties or on the reserve system than did the pacification of the Indian tribes in his day and the removal of such inter-tribal violence as that between Cree and Blackfoot.[10] Second, custodial protection of Indians—to the extent that this was an aim in the setting-up of reserves, whether by Treaty or otherwise—was of secondary importance. A prominent church worker among the Indians, who is now a bishop, has said that "very many persons supported reserves and rationalized their reasons when the underlying motive was economic—and they did not face the fact." This helps to explain why Christian missionaries assisted as witnesses during the transactions of Treaties. But the fact which they did not face was often quite explicit. The classic text on this whole subject is that of the Honourable Alexander Morris[11] who, in his account of the first Treaties directly negotiated by government, states the prime objective with cynical elegance and lucidity:

> In consequence of the discovery of minerals, on the shores of Lake Huron and Superior, the Government of the late Province of Canada deemed it expedient to extinguish the Indian title and in order to that end, in the year 1850, entrusted the duty to the late Honourable William B. Robinson, who discharged his duties with great tact and judgment, succeeding in making two Treaties,[12] which were the forerunners of the future treaties and shaped their course.[13]

Morris proceeds almost at once to quote Robinson's explanations to the assembled Indian chiefs-in-council concerning already ceded lands of good quality which were *"also occupied by the whites in such a manner as to preclude the possibility of the Indian hunting over or having access to them".*[14] In other words, the Treaties were pushed through so as to secure *primarily* the interests of whites. It is dishonest to pretend otherwise. And when we face that fact, we recognize its *human* meaning—that whites were treating Indians not as ends but as means. This denial of human equality, this assumption that the Indian is excluded from the circle of our full respect for other human beings as persons, is the most basic consideration in any assessment of the situation of Indians. It is this implication that Indians are somehow inferior that embitters these people, discourages them, and makes their responses to the challenges of the present day half-hearted, apathetic, or even hostile.

That human meaning becomes still more intelligible when we consider that this concentration of Indians in reserves fragmented them, caged them in, destroyed the conditions for a more effective intercommunion of Indian tribes for which the Rev. John West had fought, put the Indian people on the sidelines of white Canadian progress and change, and condemned them to several generations of decay. This development-in-reverse underlies our current attitudes of condescension to Indians and often of dislike and contempt. "Men kick up a dust and then complain they cannot see"; we, for our part, self-righteously lecture the Indian for his inability to master a situation that we ourselves have rendered desperate and have unnerved him from coping with.

We are back at our starting point: as Roy Taylor said, Indian incentive is killed. But, though generally speaking, the white man is responsible for this, he still does not recognize his responsibility.

It is the Indian, he believes, who is being irresponsible. And the belief that the Indian is a bum underlines the current indifference to him and the prejudice against him. Most whites, of course, are just indifferent. But in those areas of the country where the Indian does not remain out of sight and out of mind, he can, and often does, even today suffer an amount and a degree of prejudice that still deeply disturb him. The Puritan attitudes of the affluent and culturally dominant white group usually imply a strongly adverse judgment of those of different heritage and ethnic background when the latter fail to support themselves and when this failure in economic self-help seems joined with inertia; in the case of the Indian, this usually adverse judgment is confirmed by a long experience of mutual misunderstandings. Finally, the pressure now beginning to be exerted on the Indian to aspire after certain goals that the breaks in his chain of opportunities hardly allow him to reach is building up both frustration and aggression, reinforcing in him a sulky reserve or evoking from his white neighbour a racially hostile response, however indirectly expressed.

---

[1] In a strictly legal sense, Indians were never "wards" of the federal government. But it is not incorrect to say that they were treated as wards, and even under the revised Indian Act there are still some features of Indian legal status that very closely resemble the features of legal wardship.

[2] Indians are persons legally defined as Indians under the British North America Act of 1867 and the Indian Act of 1951. No child is deemed to be an Indian child unless its father is legally "registered" as an Indian. The Branch of the federal government that administers the "affairs" of Indians is the Indian Affairs Branch, as distinct from the Northern Administration Branch which includes the "affairs" of Eskimos within its purview. The Eskimos' experience of government is much more recent than the Indians', since Eskimos came under effective government attention only in 1954. In that year the Department of Northern Affairs and National Resources was set up, with the aforementioned Northern Administration Branch as a constituent. Since the early part of 1966, however, the Department of Northern Affairs has been reorganized. It has taken over the Indian Affairs Branch from the Department of Manpower and Immigration—or rather from its predecessor, the Department of Citizenship and Immigration (at one time, Indian affairs were even a responsibility of the Department of Mines and Technical Surveys!). The department retains, however, the responsibility for northern—including Eskimo—affairs. In its new form it has been re-entitled the Department of Indian Affairs and Northern Development and will function as an integrated department for native affairs.

[3] Federal administration of Eskimo affairs in the northern part of the province

of Quebec is an exception to this statement which is explained in Note 9 below. But the general truth of the statement was demonstrated in 1949 when the colony of Newfoundland became the tenth province of Canada. It appears that, in the distractions or haste of the Confederation parleys, the negotiators forgot to raise the matter of federal "wardship" of the Indian groups surviving in mainland Labrador. Though the Newfoundland government later remembered this point, it found—to its chagrin—that regular federal grants for Indian welfare were not going to be provided retrospectively by Ottawa.

4 There is one important exception to this remark. Many of the half-breed Indians who, on the prairies and in Ontario, are still called Métis, preferred to accept a once-for-all cash settlement at the time of the Treaties and therefore were never put into the register of Indians or placed on reserves. Many of the Métis were involved in the two rebellions of Louis Riel, himself a Métis. The protest of these Métis was born of the recognition that settlement of the West by immigrant whites was fateful not only for the Hudson's Bay Company and the fur economy but, as far west as the Rockies, for the Indian tribes themselves. After the second rebellion in 1885 (the first was in 1869), Riel was executed.

5 The *first* of the Indian Treaties—the so-called Selkirk Treaty of 1817 which was closely bound up with the Red River Settlement and therefore indirectly with the genesis of the Red River School—was strictly speaking a *private* treaty.

6 Canadian citizenship does not depend on the possession of the franchise or vote—unlike the situation to be found in European democracies. People can be citizens of Canada by virtue of having been born within Canada. Being equal in their possession of Canadian citizenship, they are not necessarily equal in rights or privileges. In certain areas of Canada Indians may not vote at provincial elections while the Métis may; in certain other areas, women cannot vote nor can those who do not own property. We have therefore to talk, not of Canadians who do and other Canadians who do not enjoy citizenship privileges, but of Canadians enjoying more or fewer citizenship privileges. For some of us, these ideas are difficult, nor are we greatly helped to be told that the one essential and universal privilege of Canadian citizens (including Canadian Indians and Eskimos) is that they can hold, or be included in, a Canadian passport!

7 During 1964-65, only fifty-one Indians benefited from band loans. The loans averaged less than $1,000 apiece and covered such items as farm machinery and equipment, cattle, horses, land, truck and vehicle repairs, and household furniture. Winter Employment Programmes are ignored here, since they are palliative in aim and effect.

8 Estimates of the number of these vary from something over sixty thousand to as many as two hundred thousand—the latter being also the approximate number of "registered" Indians.

9 The case arose when the Government of Quebec refused to pay relief cost for Eskimos after March 31, 1933. Accordingly, the Attorney General of Canada referred the matter to the Supreme Court of Canada (Order in Council P.C. 867 of April 2, 1935) in the following terms: "Does the term 'Indians' as

used in head 24 of Section 91 of the British North America Act, 1867, include Eskimo inhabitants of the Province of Quebec?" The answer of the Supreme Court (Decision 104, 1939) was "yes". As a result, a general responsibility for administering the affairs of Eskimos in northern Quebec came into federal hands—a process of transfer which the recent Lesage government of Quebec began to reverse.

[10] It was the R.C.M.P. that dealt adequately with both situations.

[11] Alexander Morris, *The Treaties of Canada* (Toronto: Belfords, Clarke, 1880).

[12] The so-called Robinson Treaties of 1850, covering Indian groups on the shores of Lakes Huron and Superior.

[13] Morris, *op. cit.*, p. 16

[14] Morris, *op. cit.*, p. 17.

CHAPTER 6

Despondency and Hope

The century that elapsed between the Union of Upper and Lower Canada in 1840-41 and the end of World War II is the saddest part of the story of Canada's native peoples. Paradoxically, it was a century when the Christian Churches were giving more attention to the Indians and Eskimos (and especially at first to the Indians, who were nearer at hand) than at any previous time. This paradox must be explained.

Briefly, the explanation is this: The bulk of the white settlers and the increasing number of immigrants were too busy about other things to bother about the original inhabitants. Those whites outside the direct service of the Churches who did find it necessary or advisable to pay some attention were chiefly the people who found the original inhabitants to be obstacles to be cleared from their path.

At that time most Canadians were busy about things they still can be busy about: settling the land, farming, ranching, opening up mines, exploiting timber resources, developing communications (especially transcontinental railways and telegraphs), establishing trade and commerce, towns and cities, and many related things. In addition to these economic concerns, and often closely related to them, were their political concerns centring on self-government but aggravated as ever by the "Anglo-French" rivalries, closely tallying with the divisions between Protestant and Catholic. Nor was this all. Though the C.P.R.'s and Intercolonial Railway's bond of steel was destined to unite the new Dominion "from sea to sea", there were, from 1865 on, alarms and incursions from American immigrants, whisky-traders, and soldiers who were either challenging the Canadian border at the forty-ninth parallel or driving hostile Sioux Indians (Sitting Bull included) into our prairies for asylum or disturbing the prairie Indian groups with their intrigues.

Another—and, from our point of view, a central preoccupation of that time was Canada's need for more immigrants and the need of those immigrants to establish themselves economically as quickly as they could. Few people, if any, will deny that it was part of the task of Canadian statesmanship to find a place for immigrants from the Old World:[1] it even became a moral duty to open wide spaces to immigrant settlement after the Great Famine of the 1840's consequent on the overpopulation of Ireland. Few people too will deny that, after Confederation, the Canadian government was faced by major tasks of economic and political development, external relations, and law enforcement—and the R.C.M.P. is to be especially commended for having performed, in relation to the native peoples, a thankless job with great reliability and trustworthiness. The question, however, that insistently arises is whether the federal government was acting rightly or wisely in establishing reserves. Reserves are not, of course, a Canadian invention; the Imperial Government in London had, from earlier times, regarded the creation of reserves as reasonable policy in several colonies and dependencies. But in the Canadian context the institution of reserves must probably be viewed, on the one hand, as calculated to alienate the Indians psychologically and, on the other hand, as a technique for avoiding a problem rather than of facing up to it.[2] Certainly, the psychological withdrawal of the Indian people was a feature of the Treaty period (and it has persisted), while what Alexander Morris called the "reserve system" has proved to be a very short cut with a long and miserable aftermath.

There is great irony in Morris's use of the word "system"; for, though we have used the word ourselves, it is really inapplicable to the Indian reserves. The reserves are not intended to be interdependent or to form a whole or to link themselves naturally with the remaining ninety-nine per cent of the Canadian land surface. They are intended to be, and they are, isolated enclaves of territory reserved to people of a certain ethnic character and legal status to whom certain privileges attach and upon whom certain disabilities are imposed and who, if unable to depend on their own efforts for survival, are made dependants of the federal government. When a primary function of the Indian Affairs Branch is stated to be to administer "the affairs of the Indians of Canada in a manner that will enable them to become increasingly self-supporting and independent members of the community", we have to point out that, until after World War II, virtually the only community the Indians knew was their reserve and that we offered them there, even in the material sense, precious little by comparison with others. The reserve was, of course, home for them, and there were the usual satisfactions that come from attachment to "the old people" and to a particular locality. But by the end of World War II, the young people were still almost entirely unequipped for trying their luck away from home or for becoming at home somewhere else. For the Indian people, "the split of humanity" was an established fact. Year by year the economic and social gap between them and other Canadians was growing wider; the pace of change outside the reserves was accelerating; but, incapsulated from these changes, they had no need to respond to them and, in any case, were more and more disabled from making a response.

In favour of the reserves, it is often argued that Indians are the strongest supporters of them. This is a conclusive enough argument for not now cancelling the Indians' rights in their reserves. But their attachment to the reserves does not imply that they would have been worse off without them. Prisoners have been known to love their chains and the broken-hearted to love despair. What did the Indians get—and what did they surrender—when they consented to go on these reserves under Treaty?

1. They surrendered all their right, title and interest in the lands outside their reserves.
2. They retained permission to hunt, fish and trap over the ceded territories except on land occupied by other Canadians or companies, and subject to government regulations.
3. They were granted the perpetual payment of annuities of five dollars to each Indian who is not a Councillor or Chief; fifteen dollars to each Councillor and twenty-five dollars to each Chief ("thus making them in a sense officers of the Crown"); in addition, "suits of official clothing for the Chiefs and head men, British flags for the Chiefs and Silver Medals".
4. "The allotment of lands to the Indians, to be set aside as reserves for them for homes [and economic] purposes, and which cannot be sold or alienated without their consent, and then only for their benefit; the extent of lands thus set apart being generally one section for each family of five."

In addition, some of the Treaties provided for the grant of agricultural equipment, or cattle, or fishing, hunting and trapping equipment, or twine and ammunition.

Without a doubt, however, the most valuable provision of the Treaties—not written into all of them, but now a regular feature of government service—is for formal schooling, available to the young according to the Protestant or Roman Catholic affiliation of their parents. For schooling is an aspect of the total process whereby people—and, in a country such as Canada, especially the less developed people who are of distinctive cultural background—may come to feel at home in the wider society and become equipped to cope with it on terms that do not violate their integrity. The building up of school facilities for Indian youth—even though we shall later subject the provision to a critical review—has been the most hopeful development of the last century. We must, however, be careful not to regard schooling as logically tied up with reserves. One of the oddest of the phenomena connected with defence of the reserve system is that apologists will isolate for praise certain features of life which do not require, for their existence or enjoyment, that people should live on reserves. As Canadians we can go to school without being reserve-dwellers just as we may surrender title to land without thereafter suffering a "local residence requirement" on a reserve.

Nevertheless, the expansion of formal educational facilities has had positive value for Indians during a period which, for these people, was largely one of decline. We have already seen that it was originally to the Churches that the Indians had to look for such formal schooling as they got—first through the Jesuit schools of Quebec and later through the Protestant schools pioneered by the Anglicans. But the connection between missions and the provision of schooling is only one aspect of the Church's concern in this area. That concern is not—or ought not to be—diminished as the State takes over more and more financial, administrative, and educational responsibility. On the contrary, the need to spell out answers to the Church's questions about the real nature and achievement of modern schooling for Indians will be taken up afresh in Chapter 7. But aside altogether from this, the Churches have rejoiced that the government should have been willing to assume burdens of educational supply beyond their own strength and competence.

From this willingness has come the impressive multiplication of schools, school places, and types of provision which have been so marked a feature of the last generation even though in the later nineteenth century developments were slow to get under way. It forms a silver lining to the otherwise dark cloud of Indian experience since Confederation. Statistics do not tell everything, good or bad. In particular the statistics below, while they indicate several important purposes of publicly supported schooling for Indians, conceal the problems mentioned in Chapter 3. But the statistics at least demonstrate that, in the matter of Indian education, the government has shown perseverance and a strong sense of its own priorities. Especially the educational purposes they reveal have very great interest when related to the purposes behind the setting up of reserves.

In the first place, the Indian Affairs Branch has consistently maintained an expenditure on education which is in excess of one-half of its general budget. In the second place, it has consistently increased the numbers and proportions of students occupied in post-elementary education and training. In the third place, it has plugged away at remedial education for those whose earlier schooling inadequately equipped them to establish themselves in a modern economy. Finally, the Branch's Education Directorate has vigorously pursued a general policy of amalgamated or integrated schooling, i.e., a policy that aims to bring more and more Indian boys and girls into the same classrooms as whites.

These points are illustrated by the following figures:

Indian Affairs Branch 1964-65

Total Expenditure $64.76 million
Educational Expenditure (= 55.2% of the foregoing) $35.79 million

Enrolment of Indians in Provincial and other Institutions
for Formal Education or Vocational Training
beyond the Elementary School Level

	1960-61	1964-65
High schools (Grades 9-13 inclusive)	2,021	3,993
Universities	60	88

Teachers' training	13	24
Nurses' training	18	20
Training of nurses' aides	23	74
Other vocational training	333	919

Notes: (1) 76 Indians completed training-on-the-job under contracts whereby employers are paid by the Branch "a stipulated share of wages during a period . . . agreed upon as being necessary to bring out the full earning capacity of the trainee".

(2) 562 Indians attended upgrading classes to enable them to qualify for admission to vocational training; a programme of the Federal-Provincial Training Scheme may be open to students who can achieve Grade 8 standing.

(3) In order to provide guidance services, the Indian Affairs Branch "has increased . . . its staff of educational specialists, supervising principals and teacher-counsellors. A guidance handbook for teachers was produced and used experimentally. It is planned to place a revised version in all Indian schools for the use of teachers. To assist and promote the guidance programme, a small professional library of books on guidance and testing was set up in each Regional Office."[4]

Indian Students attending non-Indian Schools (Approx. Figures)

1960-61	*1964-65*
11,000	25,000

Residential School Boarders attending non-Indian Schools

1958-59	*1961-62*	*1964-65*
737	1430	2704

In 1964-65, 57,281 Indian students were at school; 44 per cent of these (25,223 students) were attending provincial and other non-Indian schools: in British Columbia the percentage climbed to 51. Residential schools and hostels accommodated 19 per cent (10,812); Church-administered schools 13 per cent. More than a quarter of those in residential schools and hostels, Church-administered or otherwise, were actually studying elsewhere—in non-Indian schools, provincial or private.

This chapter began by pointing to a paradox—that the saddest part of the story of Canada's native peoples belongs to a period when the Church was giving them greater attention than at any previous time. But there is another paradox. As the State has sought to segregate the Indians on the reserves, it has sought to integrate them in amalgamated classrooms—as though what it did with its left hand it had to undo with its right. The State now appears to regret the institution of reserves and to be seeking—almost desperately—for devices to offset their consequences. The reserves, we said, were never intended to be interdependent; but their interdependence is now to be governmentally organized through eight Regional Indian Advisory Councils. The reserves, we also said, were never intended to form a whole; but their unification is now to be attempted through a government-sponsored National Indian Advisory Board on which each Council will be represented.[5] Finally, we said, the reserves were not intended to link themselves naturally with the rest of Canada; but the bridge-building is now to be ensured through Joint School Agreements and other arrangements for the accommodation of Indian students in non-Indian schools.

Education, it seems, is to be the "major key" for overcoming the psychological alienation and cultural retardation of Indians, consequent upon the reserve system of life. In particular, amalgamated or integrated schooling is to be given the job of increasing Indian interest in community life and development. With the improvement of communications, the residential school is to be more and more replaced by the school bus, but most of the original ideas behind Church-pioneered residential schooling are being reintroduced: Indian unity, equality of Indian and non-Indian educational opportunity, education for leadership and for "native agency in carrying forward the work of reformation",[6] streaming of school children and provision to the academically less gifted of training in the practical "arts of civilized life".

The ideas of the Rev. John West and the Rev. Peter Jones, although they have not been fulfilled in quite the ways they expected, have functioned as a "seed-bed". They have been used by the government, even if belatedly, in its own efforts at reforming the vices of the reserves it instituted.

[1] At a time when the Indian population of Canada had fallen from an estimated 200,000 at the end of the eighteenth century to about half that number by the turn of the twentieth, the Canadian government was having to try to open up the natural resources of the country to the following annual groups of immigrants:

Year		Number
1904		146,266
1905		189,064
1906	(9 months)	124,667
1907		262,469
1908		146,908
1909		208,794
1910		311,084
1911		351,237
1912		402,432
1913		384,878

In those ten years, twenty-five times as many immigrants (2,530,799) reached Canada as formed the total population of resident Indians. A mere hundred years earlier, the Indians had been as numerous as the white settlers of Upper and Lower Canada—French and Anglo-Saxon combined.

[2] One aspect of this problem is the continuing set of claims by Indian bands or tribes for settlement of outstanding land disputes. These will now have to be adjudicated by an Indian Claims Commission, which faces a particularly difficult land dispute in British Columbia. The federal government has prepared "An Act to Provide for the Disposition of Indian Claims" (Bill C-130).

[3] Even so successful a man as the late Chief Mungo Martin, the great carver of totem poles, thoroughly familiar with the city and on speaking terms with some of the most distinguished members of modern society, always felt himself a stranger when away from the reserve. There is great pathos in the words spoken in 1953 nine years before his death. He had just held a great potlach in Victoria to which he had invited the other chiefs of the Kwakiutl: "Now, now we are finished. That is the way I wanted you to come. Thank you, thank you, chiefs. You have put strength into me. For I was very sad all by myself away from home. I almost cry sometimes when there is no one here to help me."

[4] Report of the Indian Affairs Branch for the Fiscal Year ended March 31, 1962, p. 28.

[5] See report on the first Federal-Provincial Ministerial Conference on Indian Affairs at Ottawa, October 29-30, 1964, in Report of Indian Affairs Branch for the Fiscal Year ended March 31, 1965.

[6] It is, however, disappointing that only ninety-four Indians, or 7 per cent of the professional labour force, are as yet teaching their fellow Indians in federal Indian schools. There are, however, many other Indians teaching in non-Indian schools.

SECTION II

CHAPTER 7

Education and Indian Advancement

In the last two chapters, the idea of Christian missionary enterprise has been seen to link itself, on the one hand, to the processes of education and, on the other hand, to the development of a challenging community life. Community development, however, is itself one of the processes of education, while education affects and conditions the development of the community. The community may be the locality, the region, or the nation. The education will be everything occurring through the institutional life of society which will enable the young to absorb the attitudes, values, knowledge and skills that lead to adult competence, cultural at-home-ness, economic self-support, and social usefulness. Looking at matters in these ways, we can see that the Church is one of the institutions which, in our type of society, is inevitably concerned with education, is inevitably involved in certain educational processes, and may be engaged in the operation and administration of schools. Even if the Church is not active as a school agency in its own right, it cannot escape having ideas and hopes about schooling.

How, to begin with, would the Churches spell out the purposes of Indian schooling?

The Churches, we may assume, would insist that religious and moral significance ought to attach to it. We may also assume that the Churches would not want to limit this significance to the religious instruction and assembly periods of the school time-table. On the contrary, we may assume that the Churches would hope that schooling could involve an awakening of the human being to all aspects and features of the real world—the invisible as well as the visible, persons as well as things,[1] emotions as well as ideas, the beautiful as well as the useful. In this way the integral connection of the material and spiritual would become manifest to the growing child. One or two things would follow from this.

First, schooling would aim at increasing to the greatest practicable extent a young person's direct experience of the world—or rather of that particular part of the world into which he has been born. Books would be very important, for ours is a civilization that uses vast numbers of printed words. But books would never be allowed to become a screen between the student and his world. An Eskimo or Indian, learning to read, is not well served by a reader that tells of markets and buses. The world of nature around him provides material enough—or if that should run short, there is always his folklore.

On the other hand, the young person's world—a world of expanding horizons as he grows up through school—should not emphasize *things* to the point where, though he can see them, he cannot talk about them. We all know that words and things should point to each other, that language should reflect reality. But we do not all endorse the importance of verbal skills *matching* the skills of observing and reflecting on the facts of experience.[2] Someone once said that we fail to educate the young to be educators; and, if true, this is sad. When the young grow up and become parents in their turn, they ought to be able to share the educational task with the teachers of their own children. If their vocabulary is poor, if their direct experience of the world has been impoverished, if they have not learned to be sensitive in the use of words, they will be less effective. Hence, the importance of the drive for libraries for Indian communities (see Appendix II). If Indian parents find themselves lost for words, they may fail to nourish the child's natural sense of wonder and reverence. And without this nourishment the religious sense itself may never be properly awakened. Again we may assume that the Churches would not dissent from that, even though it seems a far cry from the more immediate interest of how the school can equip the young person with information and training relevant to a job.[3]

A second implication is just as important. Teaching—like the missionary enterprise itself—involves a direct relationship between human beings. In teaching, the relationship is between teacher and student; presumably the Churches would agree that, when this relationship is of a kind we can call Christian, so much the better for the education that will occur. In a word, teaching must be based on a true view of human nature. In the student's relationship to his teacher, his need is to feel that he is liked, that the cultural contribution he brings is respected, that his "weakness and waywardness" can be supported and checked by a discipline conformable to his own sense of fairness—in short, that he is in an orderly world at whose centre is something friendly and helpful. In a world like this are found the seeds of religion. Scholastically, its flower is intellectual understanding.

If these one or two points indicate correctly what the Churches are looking for *first and foremost* from the school experience, we cannot help wondering how well these purposes are being served in the schools, even though the answers must be impressionistic.

What reply, for instance, would be given by the Churches concerning their own measure of success in securing the religious and moral ends of education in the schools they administer? These are the Indian residential schools. In principle, these schools are able to form little communities where people can come to "know each other in that which is eternal". But time is necessary for such mutual knowledge. Nowadays, membership of the residential schools depends on a rationing system, under which students are allowed turns of only two or three years apiece. But this period might serve, were it not that many find their way into the residential schools because of an unsatisfactory home situation. Perhaps their parents are separated or have to leave home for long periods on the trap-lines or perhaps one of the parents is hospitalized or disabled or dead. Whatever the precise circumstances, children from such backgrounds come into residential schools with the disadvantage, which at least it takes *time* to overcome, of an abnormal and emotionally disturbing life experience. The measure of success in securing to these young persons the religious and moral ends of education must, in general, be restricted.

The same may be said about the measures of success in educating the young at school to be educators in their turn, through providing a direct knowledge of things and training in sensitive use of the words referring to them. This restricted success, of course, marks non-Indian schooling also. Everywhere we see evidence of persons graduating from school poverty-stricken both in words and in direct experience of reality. Such persons, when they become parents, will be inadequately equipped to pass on to their children, through the home, the culture of which they should be the prime transmitters. Among Indian parents, transmission of the culture learned at school will be doubly difficult, since so many Indians must forget their native language[4] when they enter school and instead must learn a foreign language—English or French. This double difficulty—first, of learning a foreign language and, second, of being educated (unlike their forebears) without direct reference to things—may help explain the relative failure of many contemporary Indian parents to transmit effectively the *non*-Indian culture to which they were introduced in their own school days.[5] In these circumstances, the gap between the home and the school can widen more and more.

Some people, however, believe that if the Indians can only get plenty of schooling, they will have opened to them the golden gates of the future. Hardly any view could be more pathetically wrong—as the studies of George A. Boyce in the U.S.A. and of Father Renaud in Canada have shown.[6] It assumes that there is some sort of magic in being inside a building called a school. But the truth is that whatever magic occurs inside a school building comes from the opportunity given to the student to confront those aspects and features of a familiar reality which he needs to understand or with which he has to try to come to terms outside the school. As George Boyce has said, success in "in-school learnings" depends "very much upon the kind of out-of-school learnings or experience which the child has or doesn't have."

From this we may reasonably infer that there will be a low level of correspondence between the out-of-school experience of students and their learning experience in school when the school drop-out rate is high. And among the Indians the drop-out rate is very high.[7] In 1963 only one in ten was reaching high school; only about one in every hundred was receiving vocational training; scarcely more than one in every thousand was entering university. These statistics conceal the fact that far fewer than the proportions of students we have mentioned completed their vocational or secondary or postsecondary education.

The following quotation, again from George Boyce, provides a useful insight into the inadequacy for most Indians of the kind of educational key they now possess; it also leads on to a consideration of the effectiveness of Indian schooling from a strictly academic point of view:

For those Indian children who come from homes deep in Indian country, who are socially or geographically isolated, or economically handicapped —often with special social welfare problems—the alarming fact is that such Indian children experience more and more academic difficulty as they advance through the elementary and secondary grades.

. . . up through the second and third grade the medians of academic achievement for Indian children of every tribe compare quite favourably with published medians on standardized tests. Thereafter, the medians of Indian children fall increasingly below the published norms. By the end of the elementary grades the characteristic pattern is for Indian medians to be several grades or more below published norms. . . .

Obviously a flunking child does not have the same experiences in school as . . . an academically successful passing child. The flunking child gets increasingly discouraged. He becomes emotionally disturbed and insecure. He suffers the maximum amount of school punishments and disciplines. Soon he develops symptoms of frustration and rebelliousness. An increasing number of Indian pupils withdraw from school as they advance in grade, while those who hang on become increasingly over-age for their grade.

At the high school or secondary level, those who try high school have a higher rate of dropouts before graduation than do non-Indian children. . . .

At the college level, among the relatively few survivors who try college, only a small percentage get past the freshman or sophomore years.[8]

Though George Boyce is speaking from United States experience, every word applies also to the Canadian scene. And though he is speaking critically, he is not in the least criticizing the Indians, least of all their intellectual capacity or intelligence. He is expressing the hope that a new situation can be created as the social context of Indian schooling and he is calling for a relevance in this schooling to the context in which it is to occur.

This is a very important plea. There is no known difference in intellectual capacity or intelligence between Indians and non-Indians, yet most Indians fall seriously behind in school[9] while many who do manage to get a good education fail in the labour market through no known factor of discrimination. What lies at the root of this profound lack of success?

In this chapter, which is primarily concerned with education and schooling, we can do no more than point to one or two of the factors.

The first of these is the poor home environment. If Indians (and Eskimos) are compelled to live in tiny, ramshackle, draughty, leaky homes and lack a balanced diet and adequate clothing and proper heating, they will not be healthy;[10] they will almost certainly prove lethargic, improvident and apparently unintelligent. Once the same people begin to obtain enough of the material conditions for a complete life, they can show up as vigorous, prudent, and able people. Evidence accumulates that a good environment helps people to unleash the energies and efforts that could allow them to deal better with life's challenges. But the question still has to be faced of how to improve the environment of Indian young people sufficiently for them, as they grow up, to discover and deploy energies, *through education*, for improving their conditions and environment still further. This is the well-known problem of "take-off"—how to move forward far enough and fast enough to begin to move upwards faster still.

The second factor leads directly from education, construed as the process of schooling, to development of the community as another educational process. For this, schooling ought to be, but for Indians rarely is, very relevant. Schooling succeeds best with most people when what is learned by its means can be seen to have importance for the business of life—a business that will involve doing *some* things, and probably *many* things, along with other persons in a group or community. Before Indian schools were set up, essentially the same teaching and learning process occurred through the Indian home—the father concerning himself with educating the boy for the male role within the culture and the mother busying herself about the girl and her place within the community. Since then, for non-Indians and Indians alike, the task of training the young has been delegated more and more to the school, while (somewhat illogically) the government has interpreted the responsibility of educating the Indian young as meaning that the Indians must be trained to acquire *exactly* the same skills and knowledge as non-Indians, as though the way of life on reserves were not quite different from that in cities. Although, therefore, for most whites living in urban areas, there is an undoubted relevance between what their schools have taught them and what they are expected to do in the community, there is no such relevance for most Indians.[11] We can see that the government escaped a possible charge of discriminating against Indians when it arranged for *uniform* curricula and textbooks; but we can also see why a large number of Indians would in circumstances such as these want to leave school early. Even if a minority should want to stay on at school to the senior matriculation year, there is a risk of another and scarcely less damaging consequence—that the Indian student may turn his back on his home and become a cultural expatriate. This is not always fatal; but in principle, it is undesirable, since it means that one part of a total experience which quite naturally ought to be linked with the other is being rejected by a person. We are not suggesting that school should exactly reflect the values of the home (or vice versa). But the difference should not be so extreme as to cause alienation. As we mentioned earlier, relationships between people are of basic importance.

The challenge, then, is to develop a school experience that will help integrate the new generation of Indian youth within the general Canadian community without alienating them from their parents and disintegrating their native communities. This is just another way of saying that the aboriginal inhabitants have to be thought of, and catered for, as both Indians and Canadians. No one ought to suppose that this will prove easy, nor that it must aim at keeping every educated Indian youngster permanently inside the native community to which he was born, nor that the school curriculum must begin to include vocational classes in hunting, trapping and fishing. There are a number of things that all schoolboys and schoolgirls in Canada must learn, whatever their ethnic character or cultural ancestry. They must, for example, learn to speak and read and write either English or French (and the greater their competence in this, the better). They must learn arithmetic. Those of a practical turn must begin to learn carpentry, bricklaying, horticulture, animal husbandry,[12] hygiene, dressmaking, and domestic science. But there are other areas in which Indians might be enabled to develop special studies: their own history, certain aspects of their traditional culture, their folklore, music, dance, religion. And why should not simple economic facts be taught that will help to make clear to the boys and girls why they and their parents cannot help but get poorer when, for instance, the price of furs goes down[13] and the cost of food and clothing goes up? The kinds of things that might be done to help remedy such a situation could be outlined to the children in the classroom and discussed by their parents outside it. If fewer things can be afforded from the outside, perhaps substitutes for these things can be found or made? Or, if one kind of product is in reduced external demand, perhaps another kind of product can make good the deficiency?[14] If far too many Indians are trying to harvest far too little wild rice, perhaps half the Indians can communally harvest the rice while the other half communally build a road, erect houses, or perform other acts of public utility? The elementary instructional material that is packed away in the circumstances of life on the reserve is quite impressive, and school teachers there should be encouraged to use that rather than simply what is authorized at the Teachers' College. It will prove to be the kind of material that links learning with life, the young people with their parents, and the members of the community with each other. It is also the kind of material that makes social change possible by promoting both economic development and the need for further training and instruction.[15]

One or two more examples of a less utilitarian kind will make this point still clearer. A desirable part of the educational background of Indians which at present appears to be totally neglected concerns how they have come to be characterized by a particular legal status, the meaning and ramifications of that legal status, and the ways in which certain peculiar arrangements on the reserves express that status. Most city-born Canadians, as they grow up, almost insensibly acquire a considerable body of information about the major structures and institutions of the city, for the communications media (newspapers, radio, television and school teachers) are pouring it forth all the time. But at school, most reserve-born Indians acquire little understanding of what a reserve really is. As they grow up, they show as little awareness as do their parents that there might well be School Committees or Home and School Associations on their reserves.[16] And rarely do they receive any insight into the potential importance of the band council as a political centre for community development. The official policies of the Indian Affairs Branch *are scarcely known to those whom they affect*, and a few years ago it was a shocking and frequent complaint, when Indians were invited by the government to make proposals for changes in the Indian Act, that they knew nothing of the Act about which their ideas were being sought. The failure to use the Indian Act as educational material, in the same way as teachers in the provincial schools would use the B.N.A. Act, has been a great mistake. As a result, the Indian often grows up with a number of serious misconceptions about the features of life on his reserve. As for the Indian who moves away from the reserve, he can be quite ignorant about certain features of urban life of which the Indian Act would have given him *negative* forewarning—for example, the role of taxation.

We have been trying to answer the following questions:

(1) What kind of education will prove to be the key to Indian advancement?

(2) What width of reference should be sought for those out-of-school learnings which—we have been told—are so important for in-school learnings?

(3) What sort of environment will enable schooling to have the best chance of proving important to Indians?

Two implications of our attempt should perhaps be stressed: first, that concern for proper schooling of the young ought to lead directly to a concern for proper education of adults (otherwise, many of the gains registered among the young may be quickly lost); second, that education must be for social change (and social change must be allowed to entail the provision of still more education). If schooling of reserve-born Indians were going to lead all of them away from the reserves, there would perhaps be no compelling case for considering the educational claims of their parents. In fact, the likelihood now is that, after all the painful mistakes of the last few years, it will be chiefly the self-identifying minority of ambitious and exceptionally able young persons who will move away from the reserve. Therefore, normal school arrangements should consider the majority who will be left behind[17] and who will remain in daily contact with the older generation. Unless we are to accept the fact of a deep split between the generations or unless we are willing to see the younger generation slip into the ways of the older generation, we must provide *adult* education. Again, unless we believe that education, at the pre-adult and adult levels, should have no relevance to the local community, we shall have to help develop "a keen community life" by including attention to its affairs within the curriculum.

We are back again to the Rev. Roy Taylor's plea. How necessary that plea still is, and how urgently (for the time being) we need to gear Indian schooling to the challenges of the common life on the reserves, can be understood if we ponder the following statement:

. . . two-thirds of all native Canadians do not go beyond grade eight in their schooling. . . . About one-third depend on Social Welfare and the other forms of public relief. . . . Roughly half the Indian population . . . depend on seasonal work—fishing, hunting, trapping, unskilled jobs—for an average family income of $1,000 a year. . . . Canadian Indians and Eskimos fare even worse than Negroes in the United States.[18]

---

[1] The kind of civilization which, unfortunately, we seem to be building is one that is fascinated by the technical and scientific achievements of intellectualism and in which knowledge of human nature becomes some kind of reflection of our knowledge of the physical world. It is, in any case, a civilization in which man, with his ideals and yearnings, is not well understood and which is not much outraged by such a remark as that of the French film producer, Robbe-Grillet: "Things are things; man is only man."

[2] The general attitude is reproduced in the following incident which occurred in England but which might just as easily have occurred in Canada—at least according to a senior official in the Ontario Department of Education with whom I talked: "An old pupil of our school found difficulty in getting life and variety into the English work of her class. She suddenly remembered the free methods used by a master [teacher] in her old school who had taken his pupils outside to collect impressions and express them in words. A jet plane had just gone screaming through the sky and someone had compared the noise to the sound of tearing calico. Determined to wake up her reluctant class this young teacher took them all out into the school ground to look at and listen to whatever might appear. It was the Headmaster [Principal] who appeared shouting and scolding, asking her by what authority she was taking her class out of the schoolroom. He forbade her ever to do it again. But the pupils' compositions for a month afterwards showed the enlivening effects of this brief excursion into real experience." G. Frances Barnes, *The Friends Quarterly*, Vol. XIV, No. 10, April 1964.

[3] It seems a far cry too from the literacy training administered by the Indian Affairs Branch, as described in the Report of the Branch for the Fiscal Year ended March 31, 1965: "Basic training in literacy aims at the development of verbal and arithmetical skills along with general knowledge; functional training aims at the application of basic and advanced skills to specific tasks such as letter-writing, completion of application forms, budgeting and maintaining accounts." Some remarks by H. A. Simon in a lecture at the University of Toronto, Fall 1966, have a special relevance both to the Indian Affairs Branch programme and to the foregoing argument about "words": "A factory that takes wheat and manufactures flour also takes in vast quantities of words and transforms them into other words. Most of the working force, and an increasing proportion of the machines in any corporation are engaged, not directly in the manufacture of a physical product, but in the manufacture of words."

[4] "There are ten linguistic groups of Indians in Canada: Algonkian, Iroquoian, Siouan, Athapaskan, Kootenayan, Salishan, Wakashan, Tsimshian, Haida and Tlingit. Apart from the Kootenayan and Tlingit, each linguistic group is com-

posed of a number of sub-groups speaking related languages or dialects."
See Diamond Jenness, *The Indians of Canada* (Ottawa: National Museum of
Canada).

[5] Father P. André Renaud, O.M.I., "Indian Education Today", *Anthropologica*,
No. 6, 1958 (Research Center for Amerindian Anthropology, University of
Ottawa): "The majority of Indian boys and girls presently in school . . .will
probably bring up their children the way they themselves have been brought
up. . . . This is what has been going on in practically every Indian community
in Canada, even those that have had schools in them for two or more generations."

[6] George Boyce is Education Specialist, Bureau of Indian Affairs, Washington,
D.C. Father Renaud has served as Director General of the Indian and Eskimo
Welfare Commission of the Oblate Fathers in Canada and is now serving at
the University of Saskatchewan as Associate Professor of Education. He is
founder of the Society of Indian and Northern Education, which consists of
alumni of his educational courses for teachers of Indians and Métis.

[7] It would be unfair to say the same about the Eskimos since the public effort
to provide all of them with at least *some* schooling is very recent.

[8] G. A. Boyce, *New Goals for People of Indian Heritage* (Bureau of Indian
Affairs, U.S. Government).

[9] Though there have been marked improvements in Indian education in the
last decade, the following statistics are not yet irrelevant:

Table I—*Grade Distribution of Indian Pupils Compared to National Average**

Grade	Indian 1945	Indian 1956	Canada 1950
	%	%	%
1	35.07	26.6	13.3
2	16.3	14.8	11.13
3	14.6	13.7	10.25
4	12.12	11.7	9.7
5	9.2	9.8	9.4
6	6.16	7.8	8.8
7	4.17	5.8	8.1
8	1.9	3.1	7.5
9	0.4	2.2	6.5
10	—	1.4	4.9
11	—	.08	3.4
12	—	1.3	4.6

Table II—*Reading Retardation of Indian Pupils by Grade**

Grade	Students Tested	Reading Score	Retardation
5.3	512	Grade 4.0	1 grade, 3 months
6.3	457	Grade 4.6	1 grade, 7 months
7.3	363	Grade 5.3	2 grades
8.3	230	Grade 6.0	2 grades, 3 months

Table III—Age Retardation of Indian Pupils in Federally-Sponsored Schools*

Grade	Pupil Population in Sample	Average Chrono- logical Age	Grade Retardation
5	512	12 years 7 mos.	1 grade 3 mos.
6	457	13 years 6 mos.	1 grade 4 mos.
7	363	14 years 6 mos.	1 grade 4 mos.
8	230	15 years 2 mos.	1 grade 4 mos.

* Table taken from Father A. Renaud, O.M.I., "Indian Education Today", *Anthropologica*, Nov. 6, 1958, Ottawa.

[10] In 1920, Roy Taylor (whom we quoted in Chapter 4) commented on the poor health of the Indians in his area of Alberta, remarking "that the Indian is weak physically and in many instances cannot keep pace with his white brother." In 1958, William J. Morris estimated that Indians in the Red Lake area of Ontario suffered in health to the point where they found it necessary to use the local hospital ten times more often than the whites.

[11] Where Indians have been mixing with whites for two or three generations (as they have been especially in parts of Ontario, Quebec and British Columbia), it is perfectly appropriate for Indians to follow the full provincial curriculum.

[12] The Presbyterian Residential School at Birtle in Manitoba has been outstandingly successful in this.

[13] Since the end of World War II, the Indians and Eskimos of Canada have been victims of the same "cumulative inequality" as the less developed peoples almost everywhere else in the world. The gap between urban living standards in southern Canada and those on the reserves or in the Arctic settlements widens not only because technological change occurs faster in the cities than in the bush or Barren Lands, but because the prices of manufactured articles on the one hand and of primary products (such as furs) on the other have moved in opposite directions. In this connection, it must be remarked that, while we may rightly be anxious about the increasing cost of relief payments to the Indians and Eskimos, the total amounts received in welfare aid have in some years been smaller than losses through falls in prices. In this kind of situation where the economic gap widens between certain groups within the same national community, mobility of labour has to be encouraged so that this labour will begin to apply itself in more remunerative places and pursuits. But there cannot be a successful policy in this regard without retraining for skills, without assistance of family movements, and (as concerns the Indians) without modifying the present system which ties Indian rights to legal residence on a reserve.

[14] Some examples may be given. The Oka Indians on the Gibson Reserve have discovered in hemlock tea a Vitamin C "additive" to their cornmeal diet.

The Eskimos have cut down heavily on the cost of living by making their own clothing, footwear and headgear, while Indians, over the last few generations, have been steadily losing this useful negative source of income.

The Cape Croker Indians have recently been trying to develop the manufacture and export of rustic furniture to offset the reduced income from traditional economic pursuits. The Cape Dorset and Povungnituk Eskimos have, for years, been doing the same kind of thing brilliantly by developing soapstone sculpture and the graphic arts. And now the Pelly Bay Eskimos in the Gulf of Boothia are "exporting" ivory and antler carvings to the South in addition to maintaining for home use their manufactures of mukluks, mittens, slippers, parkas, and bone tools.

[15] For example, if an Indian group has decided on a project of road making or house building, they will doubtless need instruction in these arts. When provided for grown-ups, the instruction becomes "adult education" and when provided for young persons, "vocational" or "pre-vocational" training. In any case this training would be a direct consequence of trying to link education to the situation in which Indians find themselves on the reserves.

[16] By 1965, only fifty-three School Committees had been established. Nineteen of them were in one province: Saskatchewan. During 1967, the Canadian Home and School and Parent-Teachers' Federation will be operating its "Tillicum" (Friendship) study-action programme, with terms of reference wider than those appropriate to the present context of discussion.

[17] According to Jasper Hill (Great White Owl), the male component of this majority ought to be able to look forward to jobs in market gardens, tobacco farms, beef and hog production, poultry and fur-farming, wildlife conservation projects, and as fire rangers, timber cruisers, scalers, bulldozer operators, land surveyors and surveyors' assistants, prospectors, railway section crews, lumbermen, game wardens, commercial fishermen, park wardens, guides, and caretakers of historical monuments (*Globe and Mail*, August 27, 1966).

[18] *The Western Producer*, November 28, 1963.

CHAPTER 8

Overspill from the Reserves

At the time of the original contact between Indians and non-Indians, almost all the Indians were nomads. The transaction of treaties, the institution of reserves, and the fixing of the "legal residence" of Indians on the reserves have brought most of our Indians to a settled life. Usually, the settlements of Indians have been at a distance from those of the whites, and the reasons for this we have already seen. An actual separation of the "races" has therefore occurred. The Indians, on their 2,200 reserves, did not discover (as the Honourable Alexander Morris suggested they would) 2,200 markets among the white settlers. Prosperity declined. Disease spread. Indian numbers went down until, sixty or seventy years ago, there were only one hundred thousand left. Since then, obtaining a livelihood on the basis of 9,247 square miles of usually poor-quality land, which was all that was left to Indians from the 3,850,000 square miles of Canada, has proved a desperate business—the more so since, with the introduction of the Indian and Northern Health Services, Indian population began to climb again. "Overspill" from the reserves has therefore had to occur. The educational improvements themselves gave impetus to this overspill, causing many Indians to believe that they could "go it alone" in the city even though their school grades were quite inadequate to the enterprise. Since the later 1940's, therefore, many of our Indians have been on the move into our towns and cities. This mounting exodus from the reserves is bringing Indians physically closer to the rest of us.

In a brief presented to the Joint Committee of Senate and House of Commons by the Indian-Eskimo Association in April 1960, the Association said that in principle they were not against Indians moving from reserves to towns and cities, that on the contrary this movement would have to continue, that its impetus would increase, and that for most Indians there would be no adequate, long-term alternative to accepting the economic opportunities of modern industry, commerce, and professional employment. Yet the Association also said—and the 1961 Census has not disproved this—that "emigration" from the reserves was merely cancelling (at best) the increase of population there; that there was still more security on the reserves —no matter at how low a level—than most Indians would find in most places away from them;[1] and that we should all rid ourselves of any illusions that Indians, unequipped for city life, could cope with urban civilization, with its intense competition for jobs, its expensive environment, its demands on credit-worthiness or accumulated capital, and its social expectations or conditions of "acceptance". "There are serious hazards to the Indians in unsponsored immigration to our cities . . . therefore, a temporary breathing space in which towns and cities may organize themselves better than at present to handle the special needs and difficulties of urban Indians could well be in the interest of Indians and public authorities alike."

According to calculations released by the Indian Affairs Branch, about thirty-two thousand Indians (or 15 per cent of all "registered" Indians) were living away from the reserves in December 1964. It is not clear whether this figure takes account of those young Indian students who are boarded in private homes and residential schools, but it seems likely that it includes the considerable number of Indians who leave the reserves during the winter, if they can manage to dump themselves on urban-dwelling relatives. To make any definite conjecture about the size of this seasonal movement would be too hazardous and therefore it seems better to ignore it. In any case, we can say that the reserve-dwelling Indian population has not declined since the later 1940's and that Indians living away from the reserves are notably more numerous than in the later 1940's.

It would be a mistake to assume that Indians have been leaving reserves solely out of boredom with reserve life. Some of the young, who have had schooling away from the reserves, cannot happily settle back on the reserves. There are others too who are captivated by the city lights. But, however interesting or glamorous the wider world may appear, the call of the wider society, if it is decisive, is usually an *economic* one. Even if Indians have not become poorer while living on the reserves in this post-war world, many of them have felt that they could be better off somewhere else. In this sense, they have felt the "relative deprivation" of reserve life (to use an expression of the sociologists). On the reserves, as they know only too well, there is little employment, either in the general sense of occupation or in the technical sense of engagement to work for someone in return for a wage or salary. Those reserve-dwelling Indians who are technically employed will be found to be occupied in (not usually very skilled) work at the school, the mission, the nursing station, or occasionally the farm. Hence, the overwhelming majority of stay-at-home Indians are still self-employed persons who, if they are not housewives, are occupied in such pursuits as fishing, trapping, ranching, farming, trucking or handicrafts. Despite exceptions (such as the rustic furniture-making project at Cape Croker), Indians seeking wages on other than a seasonal or casual basis are compelled to break with the reserves. Almost as significantly, there are other Indians who, though they will not make the break with the reserves, have no alternative, in their search for wages, but to become industrial nomads for part of each year.

If more and more Indians have been getting off the reserves for economic reasons (though without as yet causing any decline in the remaining population), we may ask: How well are these "emigrants" succeeding in finding regular employment? Though we cannot pretend, within the present summary account, to produce the scattered evidence available, we are almost certainly safe in saying that between one-third and two-fifths of these "emigrants" are looking for jobs at any one time.[2] This situation, which would be regarded as intolerable if it were current among other Canadians, points dramatically to the inadequate economic integration of our Indians.

In the reserves, the state of affairs is, on balance, worse. Since the net emigration (i.e. after allowing for those who return to the reserves) is based on this unfavourable balance, some remarks on the economic position of reserve-dwellers would not be out of place at this stage. How unfavourable in general their situation is cannot be specified because of the prevalence of "self-employment". Only relief payments offer a clue. These payments have increased by 70 per cent during the last six years and now average $80 annually for every Indian, man, woman and child. Partly this has been due to rising prices, partly to higher rates. But even together these two factors cannot disguise the continuing trend to pauperization of the reserve inhabitants. For example, in 1962, *in the best employment month of the year* (August), one in every four of the resident adult population on reserves was receiving relief. More revealing still is that one in every three of the household heads in receipt of relief had received relief also *in each of the preceding eleven months.* As the 1961-62 Report of the Indian Affairs Branch comments: "The constantly shrinking demand for unskilled labour and for the traditional skills and crafts . . . has had a serious effect."

To sum up, then, we can say that, were it not for government transfer payments such as relief, family allowances, youth allowances, blind and disabled persons' allowances, and old age assistance, most Indians would not survive on what they earn. A good estimate of the proportion of total income deriving from government transfer payments is 40 per cent per family. Yet, even including these payments, the per-capita income of Indians remains distressingly small. In 1959, in Saskatchewan, this income was only $200 per year —by contrast with an average for the Saskatchewan population in general of $1,245. Reckoned in monetary terms, therefore, the Indian standard of livelihood was a mere one-sixth of that of others in the province. It would be comforting if we had any reason to suppose that this disparity was atypical of the country as a whole. We have not. In 1963, the Committee on Manitoba's Economic Future estimated that "the levels of living and per-capita *earned* income of Indians are little more than one-tenth of that of the rest of the population."

The statistics we have just offered refer, of course, to reserve-dwelling Indians, and it would be unfair not to stress that many individual Indians and families of Indians are faring far better in the towns and cities. But two qualifications should be noted. First, in urban areas many Indians are failing as well as succeeding, coming to grief as well as "making good". Since it is a question of "sink or swim" when in the city, considerable numbers of our Indians, unequipped for city life, are sinking to the bottom—casualties of twentieth-century urban civilization as their forefathers were casualties of nineteenth-century white rural settlement. Second, the anxiety and uncertainty attendant upon urban life and, even more, the assurance that, back on the reserves, there is something approaching equality of condition, are forcing some Indians home again. Though the level of the Indian's material well-being is lower, on average, in the reserve, at least the reserve is "home" and at least minimum care for all can be relied upon there.

But to resume discussion of the net emigration from the reserves, we can say that the dearth of economic opportunities there, when compared with the incomes potentially available elsewhere, is causing the post-war exodus to continue and to augment. Enough of our Indians are now permanently living in urban areas, and enough of their fellows are joining them there, for those "serious hazards" of "unsponsored immigration" to exist which we mentioned earlier and which in turn present to the provinces and many of the municipalities the challenge to "organize themselves better . . . [so] as to handle the special needs and difficulties of urban Indians". Government—at the municipal, provincial and federal levels—is worried, almost alarmed, by this "unsponsored immigration" and is anxious to cope with the situation, in the hope that a social problem of potentially grave import can be brought under control and be limited or contained.[3] The anxiety of government is based on the recognition that, as Dr. Gordon Hirabayashi of the University of Alberta has said, "the whole urban society is inevitably involved in, and affected by, all of its sub-parts". One hundred and sixty thousand Indians may wither in their reserves: perhaps this is tolerable. But bring even one-quarter of that number into our towns, or to fester in city tenements and shanty slums on the edges of cities, and that situation is quite intolerable. If the rot can be confined to the lives of Indians alone and if it can remain hidden from the rest of us, that is one thing; if it begins to affect the lives of others and becomes an open eyesore, that is another thing.

When Indians come to town, they come as strangers. They do not, however, come as *complete* strangers. The colour magazines and often the television have made them partially aware of many features of urban life. But they do not *understand* this life. They recognize the outside of things—which means that they have some familiarity with our civilization. But civilization is not culture. One can recognize a suburban home, a car, a washing machine, and a telephone without understanding what is involved in bringing all these things together in the complex of one's own life. No Indian would, of course, ever *earn* them in face of such disqualifications as lack of job training, lack of good general education, lack of perseverance, unpunctuality, irregularity of attendance at a work place, unwillingness to suffer confinement within four walls or to endure other forms of external discipline for a fixed number of hours a day, shyness, inability to take criticism and inability to speak the same language, metaphorically and literally, as other members of the group.

When we say of another human being: He does not speak our language, we mean (if we are speaking metaphorically) that he does not see things the way we do. Professor D'Arcy McNickle has said that "Reality is not an absolute state of things as they are. A meteor flashing across the sky may be, according to the observer, a portent of evil, a falling star, or a mathematical formula having to do with mass and energy." The differences arise from culture. Similar differences in understanding can occur between Indian and non-Indian in urban situations, and that is why, when the Indian comes to town, we tend to think of him as an Indian rather than as a Canadian. Perhaps the simplest definition of culture is that it is what makes one individual feel at home in a certain social environment and another a stranger. Or it is what makes a group regard one man as an "outsider" and another man as "one of them". The Indian newcomer is usually the outsider—and that is a genuine, even formidable, difficulty for him.

Another difficulty can be inferred. When a man shows himself obtuse about certain procedures of civilized society that other people take for granted (simply because they have been accustomed from childhood to observing the experience of their own parents), such a man becomes the object of prejudice. He "must be stupid"; he does not "belong"; he does not "fit in"—people will say. Even sophisticated Indians will be perplexed by and resentful of certain procedures of industrial employment—deductions for hospital, medical and unemployment insurance, income tax, United Appeal, union dues, and so forth. No one has prepared them for these things, explained them, or shown their relevance to security. They are also expected to know many other and much less easily learned things, as if they had been born into the society that places this complicated network of expectations upon them. So, for the Indian, coming to town means a long exploration of the unknown, in circumstances where the non-Indian may only too easily and quickly grow impatient of him, resentful of his time-wasting ignorance, or even frankly hostile that he should miss so many points and apparently

insist on remaining "different". This measure of prejudice can sometimes turn into outright discrimination; it can also take peculiar
forms of outrage at unexpectedly "bad" behaviour (arriving at work
under the influence of drink) or at unexpectedly "good" behaviour
(as when a man's Bible was seized and burned by his fellows because
he was found reading it during his lunch break)!

Then there are difficulties about housing. Men who *look* different
and *are* different culturally may run up against problems of accommodation for themselves and their families. Sometimes self-declared
Indians will experience these problems even when they do not
belong to a *"visible* minority" and when their behaviour is quite
unexceptionable: they will be discriminated against simply because
the stereotype of the Indian is adverse to their reputation. Hence
the problems of acceptance at places of employment become compounded by problems of acceptance into the better kind of houses
and apartments. As a result, Indians and their families find their way
into slums, congested apartments, cheap doss houses, even skid
row. What chance have Indian children of learning the blessings
and appreciating the values of Western "culture" and "civilization"
in such surroundings? And what chance have their fathers to establish themselves as dignified, self-respecting, self-dependent citizens
when urban life starts under such harsh and discouraging circumstances? On the reserves they were free and equal in their poverty:
but today, those run-down rooms in the apartment block in the
blighted centre of the city signify loss of freedom, loss of equality.
People in that part of the city are where they are because they have
not "made the grade"—and the presumption is that they will not.

Not all the difficulties concern Indians residing in the city; they
extend to Indians visiting the city for shopping and entertainment.
Among Canadians in general there are various cultural sub-groups
—the differences between them being based on such things as income, social status or prestige, recreations engaged in, clothes worn,
vacations spent. These differences, and others of a similar kind,
express something more significant than language competence or
training and education. Since they separate even white Canadians
one from another, it is much more likely that they will separate
the "unsponsored" Indian visitor from all the sub-groups in question
except the lowest. If the Indian finds himself meeting white Canadian society at the level of the lowest sub-cultural group and class,

it may be for no other reason than that only there can he find acceptance. There the dignity is not too tight to be unbuttoned, or the shirts too white and well-ironed for downtown "binge and bingo", or the step too delicate for Saturday night's broken beer bottles. In one Ontario town a few years ago, there was, literally, only the beer parlour where the Indian could go to rest his legs, drop his parcels, and get toilet facilities—apart from a small general store on the town's remoter outskirts where one might perch on a high stool and drink a Coke.

In circumstances such as these, which deeply offend self-respect, Indians may easily "go off the rails". In Chapter 10, we describe the type of situation that was familiar at Kamsack in Saskatchewan. An Ontario community that fits well into a rather different type of situation is Kenora, where a fairly large number of Indians live on neighbouring reserves and to which the Indians come for private business, shopping and recreation. According to the report of Kenora's Probation Officer (April 6, 1961), 108 male and female Indians, aged seventeen to twenty-five years old, had appeared before the courts during the previous year from ten neighbouring reserves —seventy-two of them on liquor charges. Of the Indians charged, 79 per cent came from homes rated as less than good; 43 per cent came from homes rated as very poor. A wholly disproportionate number of the Indians sentenced were women, and if we compare the statistics for Kenora (less than 10,000 inhabitants) with those of Hamilton (more than a quarter of a million people *with almost no neighbouring Indian inhabitants*), we can infer—in relation to the smaller city—a serious social malaise which appears to be largely of the white man's making:

Town	Number of Women Convicted and Sentenced	Illiterates Charged
Hamilton	130	5
Kenora	260	70

The Ontario government pays heavy costs for police and correctional services. But the social situation in the Kenora area is one that can be controlled and remedied only by private persons and agencies acting in support of public authority, and it requires special action by the community, at least in the short run.

The subject matter of this chapter has carried us from Indian experience on the reserves to Indian experience in towns and cities. Indian experience on the reserves is a community challenge and, as we shall insist later on, it must be met by the community. The same holds good for urban Indian experience. However special the action may need to be, it must be *general community action*. And this means that every individual and group, and every level of government, that ought to be involved, becomes actually involved. Even if, in order to get things started, general community action has to be delayed, the spirit of general action must mark the enterprise. These remarks admit of no exceptions. They apply with particular force to the Church. Even if a particular Church should pioneer the way in service to urban Indians, a sectional attitude and interest has to be avoided. For the Church itself is part of the community; it is as committed as any other group and in exactly the same way. Only in these terms can the necessary community concern be developed and sustained.

---

[1] "A chance conversation with a stranger one Sunday in church triggered my visits. . . . Saying that she had just come to Toronto from Hornepayne . . ., she answered my question about whether she had had any contact with Indians there by saying that 'my saddest memory of Hornepayne is that of seeing the Indians searching for food and clothing on the public garbage dump.'" (Mimeographed Report on Visits to Ontario Reserves, submitted to the Board of Home Missions of the United Church of Canada by Mrs. R. S. Mills, and dated December 3, 1963, at Toronto.)

[2] The Ontario Human Rights Commission quotes an unemployment rate for Indians "eight to ten times the national average". (*Human Relations*, Vol. 5, No. 10, December, 1964, Toronto.)—Cf. Chapter 13.

[3] The Indian leader Jasper Hill (Great White Owl), writing in the *Globe and Mail*, August 27, 1966, had this to say: "This nasty business of integrating the North American Indian people into slum communities of the big cities is shameful, unfair, and utterly disastrous. It is a plan of extermination by assimilation. . . . Why do I make this claim? Because Indian people who emigrate to the cities, minus a skilled trade or good education, are doomed to slowly rot away on welfare handouts, and drift with the lowest class of people, where alcoholism, crime and social disease are rampant."

CHAPTER 9

Public and Private Agencies in a New Partnership

Section I provided a rapid sketch of some of the developing connections between the native peoples and the Christian Churches. Section II so far has briefly outlined the major difficulties that opened up for these people during the course of "culture-contact" as well as certain facilities that were developed to help these people overcome their problems. We turn now to finding out and describing more concretely how the unsatisfactory situation of our native peoples can in fact be transformed so that they become fully—and freely—participating members of the Canadian national community.

Until quite recently our native peoples have been mere objects of government policy. Their freedom must from now on be respected. Already State paternalism is on the way out. But it must not be replaced by a vacuum. The native peoples need a "positive State"—which will help them in democratic ways to realize ideals that they can truly call their own. But, as we suggested in Chapter 1, there is also need for a "positive Church", which will help all of us—Indians included—to recognize what our ideals really are. Finally, we need to try to work out the practical implications of the ideals for which, as citizens and as Christians, we should unite our strength.

To the extent that our ideals and the practical aspects of our ideals lead us to try to help our native peoples, the first condition for success is that we must become ancillary to their ideas, plans and programmes. The second condition for success is perhaps more difficult. We have to help them, and this implies an engagement to them and with them. Yet the sort of engagement we have in mind is also a sort of disengagement, of intervening while holding back. If any group can ensure this helping and caring for others with complete respect for the liberty of others, it is the Church—for the very centre of its belief concerns human freedom.

This amounts to saying that our native people want to grow as persons and to develop their community life according to their insight and sense of need, and that Church and State should help them, though in ways that respect their self-responsibility.

As a statement of purpose, this is unexceptionable. But though it should serve as the criterion, we ought also to examine the inherent practical difficulties, in order—hopefully—to diminish the degree of failure the criterion will measure.

First, helping people to grow as persons means educating them—to begin with, in schools. In such areas as coastal British Columbia, southern Ontario, Quebec, and parts of the Maritimes, Alberta, and Manitoba, the conditions already exist for integrating Indians, and therefore, as mentioned earlier, the schooling of Indians already occurs on an integrated basis. But elsewhere there remains the classroom problem of how to explore for what has been called intercultural unity. Ultimately there will be very many Indian school teachers, but until their supply can equal the demand, the exploration will involve (usually) a non-Indian teacher and Indian students. There will, however, be no successful exploration unless the teacher can create a situation of full and free intercommunication. How can he achieve this with his Indian students without manipulating them and imposing cultural values upon them that are implicit in the curriculum he has to teach?

The answer is that he can and he cannot. The problem is very similar to that which was faced by British colonial policy in former days which led to the now famous "indirect rule". The ideal aim of this policy was to provide "a channel through which new concepts of responsibility and growth could be fostered in native leadership". Hence, the degree of manipulation or interference or imposition from above was definitely restricted while the aim was maximized of helping people to be themselves and to discover for themselves the means of meeting their needs. This "indirect rule" was a compromise, but it was one that facilitated change by opening to discovery and use the techniques and agencies by which people might meet their needs better. In the classroom a similar compromise can be achieved. The student is provided with knowledge "for his own good", even though he did not ask for it; at the same time he is enabled to sense some new values which, if the teacher has been morally responsible and sensitively respectful of other values, will leave the student free to keep or change his way of life. A compromise we have called this; but nothing more can be asked for, and it will be difficult to achieve.

Second, the call for a "positive State" can easily be perverted into a recall of the "paternalistic State". This point has two important aspects. A paternalistic State will be a charitable State—it will not see its children begging for bread. And a paternalistic State will be an administrative State—well equipped to produce concrete, material results through plans and programmes (for sawmills, breeding cattle, roads, houses and so forth). But this kind of State might well be unacceptable to a free people, though overwhelmingly tempting to people in dependency. A charitable State may even prefer handing out welfare cheques to enabling people to bring home pay cheques. Presumably no social system anywhere will be quite adequate to secure everyone against at least temporary unemployment. But an immensely prosperous society such as ours could secure, and a charitable State would secure, every one of its citizens against material deprivation. Poverty in the midst of plenty challenges the social conscience. In these circumstances, the readiest response— which is the laziest one, whether made by the State or by persons or groups within it—is to send dollars and cents and other gifts. Speaking realistically, there will always be some people who will really need these dollars and cents; they will be the people for whom jobs really cannot be found or who are so old or ill or disabled or over-committed as to be unable to take jobs. For them, then, welfare cheques will be good. But for other people they will not be good enough. These others must be put in a position increasingly to help themselves, because far less disturbing than poverty itself is the aimlessness of an existence condemned to an absence of useful contribution.

Does not this lead directly to the administrative State? If, by the administrative State, we mean one that frustrates development rather than serving as midwife to it, the answer is no. But if, by this expression, we mean a State that is well equipped with civil servants, technical experts, and public employees, we have to answer, again realistically, that such a State has come to stay. We have simply to ensure that, within the framework of democratic assumptions, this kind of State really does enable people to meet their desire for change and improvement. The improvement must, however, be construed as self-improvement and the change as self-development. People devoted to "bettering themselves" rather than "growing into better persons" will always be in danger of preferring the kind of administrative State that frustrates development; it will be another function of the Church, in virtue of its central concern for freedom, to safeguard against this.

So far we have been concerned for the freedom of Indians to make the choices that express their own goals. But the machinery of organization is also very important.

The most obvious comment is that Indians should build their own organizations and that non-Indians concerned for Indian advancement should take these organizations seriously. Despite the internal struggles that have been weakening the National Indian Council, well-wishers of non-Indian background should rejoice that a national organization of Indians is at last being born and should construe the difficulties as labour pains. Perhaps more immediately important, because of increasing provincial and municipal involvement in Indian affairs, are the regional and local organizations of Indians. Twenty years ago hardly any of these organizations were in being, the principal exceptions being the Native Brotherhood of British Columbia (which had assumed many of the functions of a fishermen's labour union) and the Alberta Indian Association (ostensibly set up to resist the integration processes). Since the 1950's, however, many other Indian organizations have been created: the Union of Saskatchewan Indians and the Union of Ontario Indians are examples of regional groups, while the Winnipeg Indian and Métis Friendship Centre and the Coqualeetza Fellowship in Vancouver illustrate the groupings at the local level. The significance of these developments is that Indian agencies now exist that will help transform their choices and decisions into plans and programmes relevant to their goals. In the Indian-Eskimo Association of Canada, founded in 1960 largely through the efforts of Mrs. Clare Clarke of Toronto and the Canadian Association for Adult Education, they have a national alliance of friendly groups available to them for consultation and support (many Indian groups, a few Eskimo ones, the principal Churches, but chiefly the various agencies—public and private— whose activities involve them at some point in native affairs).

The bringing of private, volunteer organizations into the administration of native affairs is a new and epoch-making idea. In Canada, the partnership of public and private agencies is of course very well established in other fields. But so long as Indians were regarded as beaten people, "wards" of the government who had been dispossessed of the "favourably situated" lands and "far removed from us . . . over mountains, swamps and barren deserts",[1] there seemed to be no point in calling on the public for assistance—and no prospect of its being given if called for. Essentially, the situation up to the end of the last war was one requiring the paternal presence of the federal government, with ancillary ministrations from the Christian Church. All this is now transformed. The Indians are organizing. The friends of the Indians—even people who previously thought they had no business with Indians, such as Women's Institutes, Home and School, I.O.D.E., the National Council of Women—have already organized and co-ordinated their efforts, and are bringing a political force to bear.

Equally important are the factors that are bringing new public and semi-public agencies into the picture—provincial governments and municipalities which must now face the fact that Indians are again on the move (bringing their problems with them), welfare councils in the larger cities, school boards, hospital commissions, children's aid societies and so forth. As a consequence there is a change in the administrative patterns. Relatively, the federal government is becoming less important and other governments and semi-public agencies more important. It began several years ago when family allowances, widows' allowances and old age assistance were extended to Indians and administered by agencies that included the provincial government. This trend towards transfer, if not of ultimate responsibility, then of functions from the federal level to others received influential support from the recommendations of the Joint Parliamentary Committee on Indian Affairs in 1961.[2] Increasingly, therefore, the public services to Indians are being reshaped and will come to be placed on the same basis as those to other people or handled by the same agencies as serve these other people. There is a consequent shift in the centre of gravity of services to Indians in the direction of local and provincial authorities. In most of the ten provinces there are few departments of government that are not now expending time and money on Indians, with and without federal reimbursement. Examples are the Departments of Education, Public Welfare, Reform Institutions, Economics and

Development, Lands and Forests, Labour, and Citizenship. Consigning to limbo old ideas of "exclusive" federal concern in Indian affairs, the majority of provincial governments have taken measures to include Indians as citizens of their province. The chief response of municipal governments so far has been to take out a considerable financial investment in local Indian and Métis Friendship Centres.

This brings us to consider the city—which is the point where the developing concerns of provincial, municipal, and even federal authorities meet. It is also the point at which the private agencies—themselves established in the city—can most directly bring their contributions to bear. We shall examine the situation of Indians in the city with a view to discovering how the patterns of public and private partnership can best be arranged and what forms of service are required from each sector. Treating the city as if it were the hub of a wheel, we shall then follow the spokes back as far as the reserves, inquiring *en route* about the most desirable forms of contribution by the federal and provincial governments to reserve-dwelling Indians who are prepared to try to help themselves. We shall close this section—and this book—by asking where the Churches now stand, what new jobs they might pioneer, what old jobs they might develop further, and whether the general role prescribed for them in Chapter 1 is, after all, realistic.

---

[1] John Woolman, *Journal*.

[2] See also Chapter 12.

Indians in Urban Situations

Much discussion of the Indian in relation to the urban community has become confused because of the assumption that an urban community is one kind of thing. It is, in fact, many kinds of things. We do draw distinctions, in our more careful moments, between cities and towns; and when we are being very careful, we distinguish also between towns and villages and between cities and metropolitan areas. But when we talk about the Indian in an urban environment, about what his needs are, and about what community action may be necessary to supply those needs, we have to be even more specific. We have to look at the town or city, consider its size, how its population is made up as between Indians and non-Indians, for what purposes Indians are living there and visiting there, which particular facilities are normally required to satisfy these purposes, whether they exist locally and whether they can be extended to Indians or must, instead, be replaced by special facilities.

Every urban situation in Canada is to some extent unique. Any group of persons, anxious to be helpful to Indians in their city or town, would need to make a preliminary study of the local situation: through it this uniqueness would become clear. But some broad distinctions can be drawn between the different types of urban area —at least from the point of view of Indians. And a further distinction of some importance, as we suggested above, concerns the duration of the Indian's sojourn in town: is he there as a visitor, as a short-term resident, or for good?

There appear to be five types of situation, and each will now be described under the name of a town or city exemplifying it, where, for several years now, there has been community action on behalf of persons of Indian background and action by the Indians themselves on behalf of community development.

From Table I we can note a number of introductory points. Relatively, far more persons of Indian background are finding their way to *small* towns and cities than to *large*. Winnipeg, for instance, which contains a greater number of persons of Indian background than any other city, counts them as no more than 1.4 per cent of its population. By contrast, The Pas has an Indian constituent numbering 30 per cent of the population. It is also evident that some cities—usually small ones—have to cater for a largish number of Indian shoppers, recreation seekers, transients and so forth. The extreme case here is the Saskatchewan town of Kamsack, with a visiting Indian population approximately 66 per cent of the white resident population. Also noteworthy are the aforementioned town of The Pas in Manitoba and the Ontario town of Kenora, with visiting Indian populations almost 30 per cent of the number of white residents. Victoria, however, is a very interesting case. Many Indians use the city, but not many live there. Yet whereas Kenora, which has a similarly small Indian population, has felt compelled to institute a Friendship House and to operate it almost entirely for the visiting Indians, Victoria has managed without one.

The following descriptions, however, will enable us to get closer to the heart of several typical situations. We shall call them, respectively, the Victoria, Prince Rupert, Kamsack, Winnipeg and Prince Albert situations.

Victoria Type of Situation

1. Where a fairly large number of Indians live close to a large city and only a small number of Indians live in it.
2. Where the visiting Indians need the city for shopping, recreation, and private business and the resident Indians (usually young persons) need it for education.
3. Where the visiting Indians can use the city without any other special help from the community than security against discrimination:
   (i) in shops and restaurants;
   (ii) in access to accommodations.

In this kind of situation, things can be satisfactory to the Indians in three different degrees, as follows (in ascending order):
   (a) where the city is more or less tolerable because of the more

TABLE I

(Note: "Persons of Indian background" mentioned below include Métis; the statistics relate to 1961.)

Cities and towns in which people of Indian background live	Approx. number of residents of Indian back-ground	Approx. number of non-resident Indians using the city	Approx. total population of cities and towns
Kamsack	Few	2,000	3,000
Kenora	Few	3,000	11,000
The Pas	1,500	1,000	5,000
North Battleford	1,500	2,200	11,000
Prince Albert	1,700	1,400	24,000
Prince Rupert	1,500/3,500	1,800	12,000
Whitehorse	500		10,000
Brandon	Few	700	29,000
Calgary	250	350	250,000
Edmonton	4,000	310	281,000
Regina	825		112,000
Saskatoon	200	900	96,000
Toronto	3,000		1,825,000
Vancouver			
On reserve	325		790,000
Other	1,000		
Victoria	300	340	154,000
Winnipeg	5,500		476,000
	22,100/24,100	17,000	4,089,000

Summary

(i) Small cities and towns, with a total of about 105,000 inhabitants, contain between 6,700 and 8,700 residents of Indian background, i.e. about 7.3% of the total population.

(ii) Large cities, with a total of about 4 million inhabitants, contain around 15,400 residents of Indian background, i.e. about 0.26% of the total population.

N.B. The number of persons of Indian backround inhabiting the villages and countryside outside the reserves is uncertain but must be at least 120,000.

or less effective support of anti-discrimination laws.

(b) where the city is quite definitely tolerable since to the support of anti-discrimination laws has been added the regular, sympathetic watchfulness of a local welfare council or council of community services.

(c) where the city is positively enjoyable because of the provision of facilities whereby (i) the Indian residents find mutual support and (ii) the non-Indian and Indian residents and the Indians visiting from the surrounding areas have the opportunity to get to know each other properly and to develop friendship.

Prince Rupert Type of Situation

1. Where a large number of Indians live at some distance from a small city or town and perhaps only a small number of Indians live in it.

2. Where the visiting Indians need the city for shopping, recreation, and private business and the resident Indians (usually young persons) need it for education.

3. Where the visiting Indians cannot get quickly in and out of the town and may frequently need to stay over for at least one night.

4. Where the visiting Indians are relatively more visible (because less "lost in the crowd") and where therefore the non-Indian majority feels itself to be more interfered with or threatened by the transient minority.

Of this kind of situation, we may say that it is intrinsically more difficult than the Victoria type of situation. Often, when a non-Indian majority finds itself too regularly aware of the presence of an ethnically and culturally different group of people, it will tend to feel disagreeably about them, to be defensive in face of them, to refuse them acceptance, and generally to make life intolerable for them in the town. In such situations, though the support of anti-discrimination laws will be a powerful help, it will not be adequate to ensure a satisfactory experience for Indians. Hence, special measures, at least for a period of years, will be necessary in this kind of urban area. These measures are likely to include:

(a) a place in town which the Indians can regard as "their own" and to which (i) shoppers can come to rest their legs, rest their children, drop their parcels, share a cup of coffee before proceeding either homewards or to the next batch of domestic business; (ii) transient Indians can come for an overnight bed; (iii) the Indians resident in town will come from time to time to be with their own people.

(b) use of the above-mentioned place in town for at least occasional social events in which Indians and non-Indians can join together on friendly terms.

(c) development of opportunities for Indian/non-Indian sporting competitions (or at least of facilities on the surrounding reserves for healthy organized recreation, so as to provide a basis for future relationship between the Indian youth of the countryside and the non-Indian youth of the town).

Kamsack Type of Situation

1. Where a large number of Indians live very close to a small town and only a small number of Indians live in it.
2. Where the visiting Indians need the town for shopping, recreation and private business.
3. Where the visiting Indians are unlikely to receive spontaneous helps from the community in general, since the community feels threatened by the conspicuous presence of this ethnically different group which culturally is different in behaviour.

In this extremely difficult kind of situation there is need, aside from vigorous law enforcement (against both discrimination and disorderly conduct), for the same measures as are appropriate at Prince Rupert, except that:

(a) there is no need for hostel accommodation,
(b) there is need for the development of a regularly functioning Indian Friendship Centre.

Winnipeg Type of Situation

1. Where a large number of Indians live in a large city for work and/or study and where also a large number of Indians— whether living near to or at a distance from the city—look to it as a transit centre and use it, at least occasionally, for shopping, recreation, and private business.

2. Where Indians, resident or transient, are not a very "visible" minority and therefore do not seem to offer a threat to the non-Indian urban majority.
3. Where the size, indifference and facelessness of the large city perhaps account for the principal problems encountered by the Indians.

This kind of situation requires not only all the responses appropriate to the Prince Rupert type of situation (though on a very much bigger scale) but also the development of a regularly functioning Friendship Centre (such as we found to be required in miniature in the Kamsack type of situation). In addition, there is need for the following additional activities:

(a) on-going, on-the-spot studies of the problems of people of Indian background when they reach the city and attempt settlement there; and a regular forceful bringing of these findings to the attention of the appropriate authorities and agencies in so far as these problems ought not to be met through the Centre itself.

(b) special attention to the needs of (especially young) people of Indian background who are coming to grief in the city, who are up against the law and/or face personal psychiatric problems.

Prince Albert Type of Situation

1. Where a fairly large number of Indians live in a fairly small city for work or for study and where also a fairly large number of Indians look to it as a centre for shopping, recreation and private business.
2. Where Indians, resident or transient, are a very visible minority and therefore are the objects of at least a fair amount of disagreeable notice.
3. Where the attitude of the non-Indian majority constitutes perhaps the principal problem of the Indians.

This kind of situation requires all the responses proper to the Winnipeg type of situation, though on a smaller scale or in less elaborate form.

The following additional communities may now be listed for their activity in relation to urban Indians, and each such community is placed into the category to which it broadly belongs. Other communities than those listed either below or above have been similarly active in the last few years; they are not, however, recorded here since the type of situation they exemplify is uncertain:

Victoria Type of Situation
   Saskatoon (Sask.)
Prince Rupert Type of Situation
   Kenora (Ont.)
Prince Albert Type of Situation
   North Battleford (Sask.)
   The Pas (Man.)

Winnipeg Type of Situation
   Vancouver (B.C)
   Edmonton (Alta.)
   Regina (Sask.)
   Toronto (Ont.)
Kamsack Type of Situation
   Red Lake (Ont.)

What has already been said will have suggested that, despite the broad similarities of response indicated by the development of what has been called (rather inaccurately) the Friendship Centre movement, different committees have organized to satisfy needs in different ways. But one important distinction has still to be made. Though a Friendship Centre may be a willed community response to a challenging urban Indian situation, a particular community may not be able unaided to support that Centre. The most important factor here would be the size and wealth of the urban community.

For example, a small city such as Prince Rupert or a town such as Kenora can hardly find within itself the resources necessary for establishing—or perhaps even for maintaining—the work with the Indians. On the other hand, a large city such as Edmonton or Toronto can. Financially responsible for the capital sums requisite for the Prince Rupert Friendship House and Hostel, as well as for certain operational expenses, has been the Toronto-based Board of Home Missions and the former Dominion Board of the Woman's Association of the United Church of Canada. Again, without assumption by the Presbyterian Church and the federal government of the heavy developmental costs of the Lake of the Woods Friendship Centre, it is impossible to believe that the work in Kenora would yet have started. In Edmonton and Toronto, by contrast, the bulk of the necessary funds for starting and running the Indian Centres has come from private sources within each city, supplemented by initial grants from federal and provincial governments. This is as it should be. Where local community resources are clearly inadequate to the task, they should be powerfully reinforced from outside; where they are adequate or potentially adequate, any outside help should be restricted to the launching operation. The widest and strongest community backing for the Centre as a community project should be aimed for.

There will be no community backing, of course, until some people get worked up, develop a conscience, and spread a concern throughout the community for what is worrying them. That Churches were in the vanguard of concern in Prince Rupert and Kenora has been indicated. We could also point in Toronto to the pioneering work among Indians by the Anglican Information Centre of the Diocesan Council for Social Service and, in Vancouver, to the strong continuous staff help to the all-Indian Coqualeetza Fellowship provided by the Anglican and United Church groups. These facts are offered partly to provide evidence that the Churches have tended to be in the forefront of urban Indian developments and partly to illustrate the point that even where community-wide response to a community challenge is aimed at, a minority may have to take the lead. It does not in fact matter whether this minority is white or Indian, Church or secular; the important thing, once the minority is in being, is that its concern be communicated and shared by at least some Indians and some whites who are capable of action. Then things can begin to happen.

The next stage is that, with a directorate established, a planned, resolute attempt must be made to penetrate and impregnate the thinking of the major community leaders with the concern in question. This is a tedious, time-consuming stage: moving these leaders in the hope that in their turn they will move the major community organizations calls for patience. The wise and prudent pioneers of the remarkable developments inside Winnipeg had to put in years of quiet, obscure work before they began to see results. If people are impetuous, they will prefer to launch out at once into positive actions, trusting to luck that this enterprise and initiative will compel other community groups to take notice and offer help. But so often this does not happen, at least to the degree expected or needed. And then, with the first faltering, there can be a quick collapse. A worthwhile community concern rarely collapses if it can be taken over at a fairly early stage by a provisional committee made up of representatives of local organizations—a committee whose *whole* original purpose is to listen to what the few people have to say who are demonstrating concern and volunteer leadership in relation to it. In urban Indian work a consequence could easily be that systematic checking of the alleged facts of the situation will be called for: perhaps a conference of Indians and Métis and of community representatives will be convened. In any event, this stage can become the crucial one, since those who handle the levers of power and influence in the community are either converted to the concern or they are not. If they are not converted, the odds are against that concern for at least several more years; but if they *are* converted, then there is both a moral obligation upon the general community to take the next steps and a financial obligation to support those steps to the limits of the community's power.

This at least is how things ought to happen and how, for the most part, they have been happening. Such community approaches to community problems, however, have the following implications for Indians and for the Churches. First, since urban Indians are part of the community, they themselves *share* the moral obligation that rests on the community, and they must be associated, even financially, with the practical steps that express community concern. Second, the spirit of general action, mentioned at the end of Chapter 8, is mandatory for the Churches. This is more than a matter of trying to ensure that, in a matter that ought to be of wide community concern, there is community-wide financial support. In a few cities where Indian work exists, the particular relevance of the Churches for inter-cultural projects appears to have been missed. By contrast, in Winnipeg there has been a small committee of four Church workers (Anglican, Roman Catholic, Presbyterian and United) working with the Executive Director of the Indian and Métis Friendship Centre in some of the educational and recreational programmes. There is no domination by any one Church. One leading Indian Centre in the United States received a great setback a few years ago (from which it has not yet recovered) when one Church tried to dominate the scene.

General action, however, to give special help to Indians who are encountering special difficulties in towns and cities reflects a belief that the usual ways by which other citizens meet and overcome their problems are not entirely relevant to the Indians. To this particular point of view we now turn.

CHAPTER II

Bridge-Building between Reserve and City

The last chapter mentioned the various kinds of urban community which are the objects of settlement or use by Indians and which as a result require development in certain ways. The idea was mooted that there may have to be general community action to meet the special needs of Indians. Where special facilities are, in fact, found to be required, this requirement will arise from two sets of circumstances: first, the nature of Western society (a creation of white men whose typical product is the city); and second, the nature of Indian culture (which, for historical reasons, has come to have physical bases on reserves). The large metropolitan city and the reserves are as different as chalk and cheese. For this reason alone, people coming from the reserve system to the city system of life are certain to meet extreme difficulties. In those communities where they are appropriate, Friendship Centres have the job of building a bridge between these two systems of life. Not always is this bridge-building function recognized. Because Friendship Centres are primarily for use by Indians and located usually in downtown areas, many whites acquire the habit of regarding the Centres as temporary refuges for Indians while they learn to adjust to the white man's ways—whereupon they will graduate uptown. Building a bridge between systems is different from that. A bridge is meant to be crossed in two directions. One end, admittedly, must point to the city and open a way to all it stands for. But the other end must point towards the reserve, and people interested in integration must enter that bridge not simply from the reserve but from the city end as well.

Of the difficulties experienced by those whites who would want to enter that bridge from the city nothing will be said for the time being; instead we shall concentrate on the difficulties of Indians who come to face the city straight from the reserve.

In the first place, for Indians the city is incredibly noisy and crowded. Only at a friendly pow-wow do those raised on a reserve expect to see a noisy crowd: in the city there are always crowds, noisy and never friendly. Friendly crowds are jolly, take their time, enjoy each other: the crowds the Indians see in the city are impersonal, unheeding, madly racing between traffic lights.

Second, for Indians the city is a heap of functionaries, a bewildering variety of individuals performing a bewildering variety of jobs each one of which seems specialized. But back on the reserves there are so few functionaries that the point and purpose of their jobs is easy to grasp. There will be a minister or a priest, perhaps a trader or Indian agent, a school teacher, a nurse, and, of course, an Indian chief who, in fact, is no more than a *part-time* specialist. Even the minister or priest, the nurse or school teacher may well finish up by being a part-time specialist. For the Indian preference is to shove extra jobs on these people, to transform them into generalists or multi-purpose activists who run the Boy Scouts, the Girl Guides, the sewing and handicraft classes, the Homemakers' Club, intervene with the Regional Office of the Indian Affairs Branch, run the sick to the hospital or nursing station, and generally arbitrate on many issues of private dispute. Even as specialists, however, they are felt to be different from city specialists. For on the reserve the specialist is known as a person; he is seen regularly and has many direct relationships with the inhabitants that have no connection with any kind of purpose. The reserve's specialists, therefore, are first and foremost human beings with whom the local population can enter into direct face-to-face connections. Among city-dwelling whites it is insufficiently recognized that most Indians still understand only primary, all-purpose organizations; that they feel uncomfortable with multiple, specialized functionaries; that the latter always constitute for them a somewhat intimidating out-group; and that the Indian response to an out-group is invariably reticent, nervous, and suspicious. As a result, officers of Friendship Centres have to take Indian newcomers by the hand to interview landlords, personnel officers, Indian Welfare officials and so forth. The impression created upon the white functionaries by all this apparent helplessness is, of course, very unfavourable. Sometimes the functionary is himself disturbed by his own lack of success in establishing a proper contact with the Indian client—a response that intensifies the painful sensa-

tions of the Indian; much more often, the functionary is quite un-
aware of how forbidding he appears to this Indian and how a natural
Indian shyness may become exaggerated almost to the point of
mental and verbal paralysis in his presence.

Imagine how the Indian will reason about his first impressions
of city functionaries . . . "Why do I, even in this same building
and office, have to be handed on from official 'A' to official 'B'?
If I am but one person with some few needs, why must I visit
different persons for each one of my needs? Am I a human being
or a set of cases? Why do those who deal with me use such long
or difficult words ('referral', for example, which I'm sure I never
learned at school)? And what on earth is this Programme 5 and
that Section 72? And where do I start looking for details about them?
Somebody said that if I phone up a certain number I will be told—
but whom do I ask for when I phone, and how would I make clear
my puzzlement, with my poor command of English words? And
isn't it very bad manners for these officials to ask me so many questions about myself? Do they think my private life is public property?
Is this one of the values of the white man's civilization—open-plan
life, to match the open-plan home design? If these people are really
so interested in my age and my mother and my father and my
religion and my monthly income (in case I have one), why aren't
they more friendly? Why do they delay their help and seem so aloof
and ask me to come back and appear unconcerned as to how I am
to manage until I come back? And why, why, why, do they want
everything I say to be written down by me—and not on one sheet
but on three?"

And so we might go on, asking the questions the Indian must ask
as he is shuttled around our puzzling cities. No wonder that to
mistrust, resentfulness, perhaps hostility, are added bemusement
and bewilderment which reinforce his sense of reserve, his diffidence,
his felt incapacity to use the white man's language. And then, in
addition to all else, the Indian may be unable to get work, or to hold
down a job, or he may be desperately short of working capital and
angry that he has to pay high prices for what on the reserve was
cheap or free; or he may not know how to budget his money and
will therefore quickly run into debt. How easily within no time can
a city Indian immerse himself in a sea of troubles, sink, give up the
unequal struggle, become one of the submerged tenth—one of the

bottom-of-the-sea people who because they are at the bottom have one thing in common and because of that one thing, accept each other, not with mutual respect, but rather in common rejection of a way of life utterly remote and impossibly demanding.

What, in the third place, makes the lot of almost every Indian newcomer to the city unenviable is that he rarely if ever arrives with a skill in short supply. Essentially he comes to the city, if not as a suppliant, then as a gambler. And he does not command the bravado which, among some whites, helps to bring the gamble off.

Consequently, the Friendship Centre—where friendly whites as well as friendly fellow Indians are to be found—has an enormous moral, educational and even material importance. Through the Friendship Centre, something is done to cushion the shock of the first days and months. Here the Indian has a place to which he can come in all situations of hardship, distress and loneliness. He will find nothing luxurious at the Centre and nothing disconcertingly respectable; but he will find it welcoming and reassuring, and the people there will be reliable in their advice, sound in the information they offer about other agencies, and ready—at least at the outset—to give a little special help in interpreting needs and making contact with these "outside" services. Best of all, the Centre is the place in which the Indian, little by little, can begin to feel himself to be part of the total community. From the Centre, which itself is as much a community institution as a YMCA/YWCA or church, the Indian will one day be stepping out to play his part as a free and equal member of the local society.

We have been stressing the "bridge" role of the Centre and have suggested that this bridge is open at one end towards the city and at the other to the reserves. It is therefore not surprising that the following functions are frequently agreed upon as belonging to the Centre:

1. Early contact with newcomers to the city, and, if possible, some kind of counselling of them (by minister, or priest, or school teacher) before they leave the reserve.
2. Finding out what the needs of the newcomers are.
3. Referral of newcomers to appropriate social service agencies, where these exist locally.
4. Providing through the Centre, if possible, a personal counselling service, as well as such information and advice as would be

appropriate to a Citizen's Advice Bureau, when special community service agencies do not exist to provide them.

5. Provision of accommodation for the recreational, educational,
and, in general, the social interests of the users of the Centre.

6. Maintenance of a registry of jobs, houses, and apartments
available.

7. Interpretation of the urban Indian, his needs and his rights to
the public in general and to the other principal community
agencies.

8. Provision of opportunity, to Indians using the Centre, to assume
responsibility for it as something that is theirs and to develop
it as a centre of Indian cultural heritage in all its significant
forms.

Sometimes it has been objected that such functions of Friendship
Centres as we have just mentioned create a "reserve within the
city". This criticism is beside the point. Experience has already
shown that among the core-users of a well-run Friendship Centre,
the turnover is once every ninety or so days; in other words, the
Friendship Centre is proving on the whole a very good bridge for
leading the Indian newcomer into satisfactory membership in the
local urban community.

In saying this, however, we should also point to two other functions of Friendship Centres which so far have proved to be beyond
their capacity, though extremely important.

1. Applying to the Centre will be many young people whose
educational and other background is such that scarcely any employment agency would consider them even for unskilled jobs. Being
still "legally resident on a reserve", these young people would fall
through the mesh of most federal-provincial schemes for educational
upgrading with a view to vocational training. Yet these same young
people have no future even on the reserves. So long, therefore, as
Indians are denied "citizenship status" by the Province and the
benefits of such joint schemes as have been mentioned, the only hope
for these untrained young Indians is that they can be encouraged
and helped to acquire a reasonable or modest competence in the tool
subjects (writing and mathematics) which they will then begin to
use in training for the skills relevant to livelihood. At present, there
must be hundreds of urban Indians in their late teens or early adult

life whose scholastic level is no more than grade 6 and who—as a spokesman of the Winnipeg Friendship Centre observed—suffer so many disqualifications that they would not be taken on as dish-washers.

2. Many young and even older people have come to grief in the city and actually fight shy of contact with the Centre. The Anglican Information Centre of Toronto, reporting in 1962 shortly before the setting up of the Canadian Indian Centre of Toronto though long after the establishment of the Toronto Indian Club, had some excellent words on the "appallingly difficult problem" presented by these people.

> They are so lacking in self-confidence that setbacks are felt with a degree of acuteness such as drives a person to drink or back into drinking habits. Drink as a means of amnesia of the intolerable is evident in periods of prolonged unemployment; in addition, other aspects of a less satisfactory pattern of life can re-assert themselves at this time. Once the improvement of morale and circumstance that may have been facilitated by the worker or some public agency has apparently been annulled by misfortune or mistake and once discouragement has again taken hold of a man or woman, even the smallest degree of self-responsibility seems to be too much. Hence, the attractiveness of gaol for some, as an ordered and secure community to which the member must conform. Helping overcome the sense of dependency and "can't make it" is the principal task of the worker with these people; unfortunately, it is such slow and insecure work that, though the number of persons to be helped may not statistically be impressive, the problem appears too large for existing resources. This remains true even when other agencies are brought in such as the Elizabeth Fry Society, the Alcoholism Research Foundation of Ontario, Big Sisters and the Children's Aid Society.[1]

These comments would be echoed from Winnipeg where the Centre has developed as its deepest concern some ideas and a working scheme that could be important for these "lost souls". A project has been suggested that would require floating case-workers on the city's streets, so that people who are near the end of their tether could be "picked up in time, and an emergency hostel could house them until sound plans could be made on their behalf (including perhaps psychiatric treatment and/or upgrading and socialization classes or the teaching of some basic vocational skills)".[2] Though nothing has come of this so far, a very promising experiment has developed since 1961 out of a joint understanding between the

Centre, the Police and the Courts concerning those Indians who actually infringe the law and who formerly were receiving short-term prison sentences in large numbers. Mrs. F. M. Bastin,[3] Chairman of the Centre's Personnel Committee, reporting on this development, had this to say:

> In many instances these people had little understanding of the legal procedures in which they were involved, and the results of [the] . . . sentences were . . . very often . . . damaging both to the persons concerned and also to the general attitude of Indian people to law enforcement agencies.
>
> In 1961 a new magistrate was appointed to the Winnipeg police courts who became very much disturbed and concerned about the existing situation. Discussion took place between this magistrate, the Centre's executive director, the police inspector and subsequently with the Board of the . . . Centre. As a result, it was agreed to extend the work the executive director was doing in the courts. She and members of the Indian Council agreed to try to help persons if they were given suspended sentences. [With the support] of the agreement, the magistrates were able in many instances to justify giving suspended sentences on the understanding that persons receiving such sentences would keep in touch with the executive director and the Centre and that staff and Council members[4] would do what they could to assist them solve their problems.

This work has now been going on for seven years.

We have, however, candidly to acknowledge that the operating scheme at Winnipeg has principally been helpful only to those Indians who come to public attention because of drink and relatively minor offences connected with drink. The hard-core problem remains untouched by the Centre's efforts—just as the same problem in Toronto has remained untouched by the Indian Club of that city. This Club—now reorganized as the North American Indian Club and functioning as a constituent of the Canadian Indian Centre—has always served as the rallying point for those Indians who have established themselves satisfactorily, both economically and socially, in Toronto. As the Anglican Information Service puts it:

> Ideally . . . the Club *could* provide some kind of focus for the social experience of those Indians who are still facing acute difficulty in adjusting to the city. Two factors, however, tend to operate against the Club's functioning in this way. On the one hand, many of the Indians who have an unsatisfactory pattern of life are not themselves anxious to make contact with the Club. . . . On the other hand, the Club itself may not be anxious to give a sustained attention to those who are con-

tinually facing acute personal difficulties. . . . For this reason, the problem can intensify itself, and the burden of loneliness (for the individual) can become heavier and heavier. Friendship and help are deeply needed yet rejected. Escape from an old way of life is desired, but not sought with that measure of responsible choice as might secure success.[5]

The problem just outlined is a fairly familiar one: many besides Indians face it in our great cities. It is a problem that those who lack professional social work training will scarcely know how to begin to handle; at the same time, it is a problem that a group such as a Friendship Centre or an agency specializing in case and group work with Indians such as the Central Neighbourhood House of Toronto is very well placed to organize and direct. It would therefore seem that the Winnipeg Centre was on the right track in proposing that the unsolved problem of these "submerged people" be tackled, not by volunteers, but at a professional level. As has been previously argued, much concern nowadays has to express itself, not in direct, personal service (even though we should always seek to maximize the opportunities for this), but indirectly in supporting the salaried work of specialized functionaries. And so long as the control of professional work on behalf of a social concern is firmly vested in the hands of a volunteer group, the resultant service is a form of Voluntary Action.

At the present time, the Friendship Centre movement—whether it is still at the local committee stage or has already burgeoned as a new community institution—offers the volunteer a wide variety of opportunities for service. When, as at Winnipeg, the Centre runs a whole series of classes and special lectures, organizes a library and working parties, promotes an A.A. group and sales of Indian handicrafts, plans dances and movie shows, musical evenings, hay rides, sleigh rides, picnics and parties, while keeping close connection with many community groups to whose activities the members of the Centre are constantly introduced, there is usually some way in which the non-Indian volunteer can participate.

Two cautionary words are nevertheless required. Though our native people need the friendship of other Canadians more than anything else, simple benevolence would not be enough. Again, though voluntary service of others usually implies a spirit of friendship to others, the kind of service a non-Indian volunteer might most want to give in a Friendship Centre might not be the service most wanted of him. A hard lesson may need to be learned by the non-Indian about the ways in which he can best help Indians. True friendship may require a holding back from doing things Indians would prefer to attempt themselves. Or it may require substituting a professional skill for amateur goodwill. Or it may require the half-joyful and half-sorrowful discipline of seeing people make, and learn from, mistakes. Whatever else it may require, it will require, above all, accepting people as they are—accepting them, not primarily as people of a different ethnic or cultural character, but really as *persons* who have worth as *persons* with personal needs and goals. Perhaps the whites can assist the native peoples to define their goals, to assess these ends as realistic or otherwise, to suggest means to these ends, and even to help provide the means. But, in general, the friendship most valued by our native peoples is what is not obtrusive, not pushed, not talkative, and certainly not sentimental. Often it seems that the best friendship is quiet listening—a species of relationship in which Indians themselves excel.[6] Often too, it is a making clear to Indians not only that they would be welcome in non-Indian homes but that non-Indians for their part would be happy to return the visits.

This leads directly to perhaps the most important point of all. If Mrs. A, an Indian, and Mrs. B, a non-Indian, know and respect each other and share certain things, inter-visitation is a perfectly natural expression of their feeling for each other and strengthens that feeling. Inside towns and cities, this kind of inter-visitation should be greatly extended. But, in addition, there is group inter-visitation and, to begin with at least, this seems to have even greater possibilities.

The types of group whose inter-visitations ought to be developed are these:

1. An urban Indian group and a reserve Indian group.
2. An urban Indian group and an Eskimo group.
3. An Indian group in one city and an Indian group in another city—perhaps using the technique of the "pilgrimage" (as happened when Toronto and Brantford Indians visited Indians in Winnipeg, Saskatoon, Calgary, Edmonton and Vancouver, on the occasion of the centennial of Pauline Johnson, the Mohawk Indian poet).
4. An Indian group (for instance a traditional dance group) visit-

ing inside the same city a non-Indian group such as an audience of Rotarians, or a non-Indian group (for instance a committee of the City Council) visiting inside the city an Indian-Métis Friendship Centre.

5. A non-Indian (or largely non-Indian) urban group and a reserve Indian or an Arctic Eskimo group.

No special points, not already covered, arise in connection with the first four types of group inter-visitation. The last-mentioned type, however, of which there have been one or two instances in the last few years,[7] has probably a fairly big future provided that the basic conditions for success can be secured. Inter-visitation is intrinsically more difficult on a group than on an individual basis, being attended by the risks that the visit will be either "strictly functional" or a mere "social occasion". When, however, the Church provides both the institutional means and the spiritual basis for group inter-visitation, these dangers are avoided: a "fellowship of reconciliation" becomes possible in a new form.

The reason why the Christian Churches could pioneer this kind of venture more successfully than any other agency is that all those who visit each other under Church auspices are united in advance by ties not depending on previous acquaintance, mutual liking and so forth. Being Christians, they would all be united in advance "by agreement as to the things they love". Linked in a common loyalty, they would meet in the flesh as an already real community of persons. There would be nothing phony about such inter-visitation— and nothing, either, that would tend to divide people into sections or cliques, as so often happens when they gather "for a purpose". Church-sponsored inter-visitation, then, is a project for which the Church seems admirably equipped and it deserves the Church's more widespread consideration.

To sum up. The non-Indian who wants to be of help to Indians (and foreseeably to Eskimos too) who come to the city has to be ready to offer them, beyond all else, acceptance. In an earlier chapter we mentioned the difficulties, disabilities, and inhibitions suffered by so many whites when they want to express a concern for the urban Indian. Some part of their problem often is that a degree of skill, which they do not possess, is needed in order that they may be helpful to Indians or win their confidence. Non-Indians too may easily offend Indians through ignorance of their cultural traits.[8] Because of this, we have simultaneously to wean certain non-Indian volunteers from attachment to over-simple procedures and to harness their enthusiasm in newer forms of activity. We must recognize that, alongside a training of these volunteers in the facts of the situation, there has to be a sustaining of their sincerity and vision. One of the sadder facts of our welfare society is that it may be unable to find a place for the non-professional idealist. It would be a pity, especially at a time when the "enthusiasm of humanity" is at a premium, if we failed to find ways and means for using good-will and if we created the impression (which automation is foster-ing in the economic realm) that only people with special knowledge and sophisticated technique are really needed in our complex world. The pity of it would be the greater in Indian and Eskimo affairs, since the aboriginal peoples of Canada have a very evident feeling for *people as such.* Certainly we must try to ensure that whites, in their first contacts with the aboriginal peoples, do not destroy, through cultural gaffes, the basis for trust and confidence. But, even more, we must be careful to believe that Indians and Eskimos have a great deal of insight into the charity of those claiming to be their friends. Concerned friends can make mistakes. But if they bear them-selves humbly and with "reverence for life", this will not escape our native people; it will touch their hearts and engage their loyalty.

---

[1] The Indian-Eskimo Association of Canada, *The Urban Indian Canadian* (Toronto, 1962), pp. 10-11.

[2] *Ibid.*, p. 18.

[3] Mrs. Bastin is a well-known Anglican who was Secretary for Christian Social Service of the Dominion Board of the Woman's Auxiliary and also Chairman of the Greater Winnipeg Welfare Planning Council's Indian Conference Com-mittee.

[4] At the Winnipeg Centre, the Council is responsible for day-by-day adminis-tration, including the Programme, and all its members are *Indians.* Indians too are represented on the Centre's Board, which for the rest includes non-Indian representatives of community agencies.

[5] Indian-Eskimo Association of Canada, *op. cit.*, p. 11.

[6] Taos Pueblo Indians, it is said, wear soft-soled shoes so that they may feel the earth. The quiet Indian social manner is an excellent way to feel persons. Non-Indians might well learn a lesson here, and, instead of abhorring the occa-sional vacuum of silence, welcome it as helpful in the conversation of friends.

[7] For example, the visitation of Eskimo groups in Povungnituk and Cape Dorset by a group of urban non-Indians drawn from Ottawa, Toronto and

Montreal and organized by the Indian-Eskimo Association in August 1962. Also, within the Anglican Church of Canada, the "link parish plan" which is developing in the Qu'Appelle and Rupert's Land Dioceses. Finally, within the United Church, the Vacation Bible Schools on the reserves help to serve the same purpose.

8 "Crash" training for the simpler skills has been a major purpose of the annual seminars on urban Indian work provided by the University of Saskatchewan in co-operation with the Indian-Eskimo Association. The Women's Inter-Church Council of Canada gave strong support to the pioneering seminar in the fall of 1963.

CHAPTER 12

Helping Them to Help Themselves

Recently the Director of the United States' AID organization, viewing the international scene and the situations and tasks confronting his agency, said in a circular letter that "the gap between central governments and rural areas has led directly to serious social and economic unrest." The same kind of unrest exists among our own Indian population. Since 1945 there has been some real improvement in the economic welfare and social opportunity of our Indians, but there has been no corresponding reduction in their sense of grievance. On the contrary, a feeling that their position continues unequal and inferior has increased their unrest. What was once probably taken for granted is now being felt as unjust: compounding the sense of injustice is the sense that they have less and less to show for their lives, in their confined and isolated situations. Perhaps a recognition by the Indian Affairs Branch that their woefully poor economic situation was rankling bitterly or perhaps the imminent sittings of the Joint Parliamentary Committee proved the decisive factor; in any case, an Economic Development Division for Indians was set up in 1960. The fact, however, that such an obvious administrative need could be delayed for so long indicates that here too there has been a gap between the federal government and the Indians on their reserves. From this gap must originate, at least in part, the "serious social and economic unrest" among Indians.

In the circular letter quoted above, the question had been put as to "what new political and administrative practices" might be introduced so that the gap referred to might be bridged. This is an interesting and still rather neglected aspect of the whole problem. Part of the answer to the question is coming to be supplied (at least if we take an optimistic view of what is currently happening) through the increasing participation of provincial governments and the use of joint federal-provincial agreements. But the gap in question is psychological. It expresses the alienation of Indians from the government that is charged with responsibility for their well-being; it marks their felt inability decisively to influence the government in whose election they share, or at least decisively to influence the administrative arm of that government into a respect for their own freedom. "The social and economic unrest", therefore, becomes a symbol of a more basic problem that goes to the roots of human personality: What measure of freedom will be accorded to Indians in developing their communities according to their own best insights? What freedom will they have to *develop themselves* and in this way educate themselves for further change?

If the freedom of the Indian within his own local community is made the criterion and central reference, the all too familiar preference of many technical experts for downgrading the requisites of local autonomy must be rejected. Admittedly, the delays attendant upon the decisive emergence of the people's will can be very frustrating; so can the reactionary deflection of people from goals acceptable both to the experts and to modernizing groups within the community. These frustrations must be suffered. In the last analysis, the institutions of local self-government (to use an old term) cannot be by-passed or impatiently manipulated. If community development is a social method by which people may be able to develop themselves, the people cannot be treated as objects of policy, nor can their local political institutions and resources be merely exploited. If community development is to have any vitality, so that the people involved can be changed through helping to change their own environment, the people themselves must play a leading role in shaping the course of their advancement.

To say this does not mean that no outsiders are to be involved.[1] The impulse to community development in the early stages of transition often comes from persons within the local social structure who have connections beyond the community. Other impulses may come from field representatives of the technical and administrative branches of government; in the context of Canadian Indian affairs, these ought to be—and are much more likely to be—the field representatives of the nearest provincial government rather than of the remote federal authority, and their influence will be felt (to begin with, perhaps only feebly) in the lowest level and unit of formal administrative authority—the band council. In Ontario, and also in British Columbia, where the provincial government has entered Indian affairs in a strong, positive way, a number of band councils have, in fact, been recognized as municipalities, and this is to the good to the extent that it increases local self-responsibility.

The question, however, still remains of how the necessary outside impulses are to be secured their proper role, and the necessary outside resources harnessed to the community's purposes, without the outsiders running the show. The attempt to answer this question must take into account, first, that this leads us into describing procedures that, so far, have not been very generally used in Canadian Indian affairs; second, that the basic conditions for developing these procedures are none the less establishing themselves; third, that the existing machinery of Indian local government—the band council— was not devised to answer the particular question we face and is not, by itself, capable (except in a few instances) of discharging the tasks of community development.

At present most band councils have two functions—as the federal government's local agency for applying regulations, and as a two-way channel of communication between the local Indians and the federal (and, increasingly, the provincial) government. The more deliberative functions—weighing matters, taking up attitudes, and deciding for or against this or that action or project—will tend to occur outside the band council, even though some of the same persons may be involved in the discussions outside and inside. These outside discussions may even be held outside the band, for example in a meeting of the regional or provincial Union of Indians (as well as, from now on, in regional advisory councils): in any case, we must assume that there will be both a formal and an informal leadership, and that each leadership will usually be in contact with the rank-and-file members of the Indian community.

But how does that kind of change or innovation occur which the Indians really want? On the usual existing arrangements, it cannot occur except on terms of *government* leadership. But another way is possible; and, for the sake of brevity, this other way is described on the supposition that what the Indians want comes first as a suggestion from beyond the membership of the band. (The reader will be able to figure out for himself how things would be arranged if the suggestion were first to arise from within the band.)

This suggestion is for some local project. It is tentative. Perhaps later it may turn into a proposal that some (temporary) organization be set up. But, for the moment, it is a bare idea, put forward by someone connected with a locally known interest group. It reaches the band council. But inside the community the idea is still no more than a seed. Nothing will happen until the formal and the informal leadership and the local community become active in a discussion, consultation, and liaison with potentially interested public and private groups. Perhaps the band council, on behalf of the local community, will find it expedient to call in the Indian Superintendent to indicate their first reactions to the idea and to elicit his own. The Superintendent for his part will have to seek to interest the Indian Affairs Branch, and perhaps through the Regional Office the provincial government will have to be approached too. If the project is one that includes the Churches or mobilizes some of their resources, the local priest or minister may be unofficially asked what he knows and thinks about it; in any event, private non-government agencies will be canvassed. By the usual channels all the answers, impressions, and advice received will be conveyed back to members of the local community whose leaders, inside and outside the council, will then reach a decision to reject or adopt the suggestion. If they reject it, that is the right of people engaged in self-government. If they accept it, that is equally their right. Any agreement to accept it must lead to the working out of a plan and programme, and in all likelihood this will entail much additional consultation, discussion, and negotiation with the outside helping agencies and with the supporting interest groups. What eventually emerges as the implemented project will therefore be the project of several institutions. Limited and specific in their ordinary functions as some of them will be, they will have acted together as one united whole to form, implicitly and for the purpose of the innovatory project, *the general government institution.* In the preliminary process, all the necessary conditions for developing the project will have been mobilized—ideas relevant to eliciting a point of view from the local community; efforts necessary for organizing the activity; and a detailed programme for it. This kind of local government is different from the one most people picture to themselves; but in the circumstances of a community in transition (a developing community) this is the only one really feasible, and it is genuinely democratic. It is actually quite close to the partnership of volunteer and statutory organizations sketched out in Chapter 9 as a desirable political and administrative practice for Indian affairs. The model we have constructed essentially consists of a series of interactions among public and private institutions whose ordinary or normal functions may be either political, administrative, economic, educational, religious, or communal.[2]

If this kind of local government links public and private agencies, it has a tendency also to link the local community with the higher levels of government, closing that gap which the AID Director had considered to be a cause of economic and social unrest. From the local community to Ottawa it erects a ladder, providing the steps whereby the federal government can really reach down into the reserve and whereby the reserve can reach up and feel itself to be part of the nation. If the ladder runs through a provincial capital, there may well be questions of finance and jurisdiction to be hammered out. But outweighing any difficulties of that sort are two very great advantages. First, the federal government is at last able, by the means described, to move away from using the band council mainly as the formal intermediary in rule-controlled transactions with the local Indians: instead, by these same means, the federal government can become responsible for Indian affairs in a more positive fashion, even if it is functionally less involved than, say, the provincial government. Second, the band council is enabled to have access to the resources it needs because no one can any longer claim that the council lacks the know-how for the projects in question: the council has annulled the claim because it has united itself, for the duration of the project, into an institutional combine or complex through which not only finance and technical aids but training facilities, expert advice, and information can come.

In the next chapter, attention will be given to the possibilities of Indian advancement by federal and provincial actions in the social and economic fields. At the federal and provincial level, the Indians cannot, of course, be as fully responsible for these actions as when they act to shape the course of their advancement at the level of the reserve. This point can be put another way. While Indian advancement at each level requires a response involving self-help and effort, advancement at the local level primarily depends on developing the group's own initiative, as distinct from advancement at a higher level which primarily concerns individuals and primarily depends on the initiative of governments. The same point would naturally hold good for non-Indian advancement; in our kind of society it is, so to say, in the nature of things. It is not, therefore, something to be worried about. The distinction that has been drawn does not mean that one type of advancement is more important than another. It means that one type is more relevant to moral and educational self-improvement aside from any material results, while the other is more relevant to the material results. The one is an expression of community development, the other of welfare.

Since federal and provincial actions for social and economic well-being are being deferred for consideration in the next chapter, we conclude the present one with further remarks on community development—it being understood that, in a material and utilitarian sense, the Indian standard of living would be much more powerfully affected by the kind of developments to be discussed later on. In this book several things have already been said which underline the necessity of the community development process despite its inability to transform the situation of the Indians without the aid of the other process.

In the first place, there is—or at least there ought to be—a close connection between community effort and schooling, partly because schooling should enable a person to make an accommodation to changed circumstances of life and partly because it should encourage and equip a person to change the circumstances of life[3] in his community. Yet despite the quite large sums already expended by the Indian Affairs Branch, the improved opportunities for formal schooling have not so far yielded—except to a relatively small proportion of energetic and intellectually able Indians—the benefits so confidently predicted fifteen or sixteen years ago. In Chapter 11 it was pointed out that many Indians are so ill equipped for change that they become social casualties of urban civilization even before community action is able to reach them. On the reserves, as we saw in Chapter 5, effort in the community for the community cannot, for the most part, be related to what is learned at school; hence schooling is not regarded as important, effort on behalf of the community is not persistent, and social change is not very apparent.

In the second place, Indians have been separated, if not completely isolated, from the main developments of Canadian life. Even before their removal onto reserves, they were culturally different. Despite the number of Indians on the move, emigration from the reserves is so far from offsetting the increase of population there that the problem of the reserves continues to grow. Many of those who emigrate cannot make a go of it away from the reserves. Though we speak of the reserves' "crumbling walls of separation", the present chief[4] of the Citizenship Branch (now transferred to the Office of the Secretary of State) had this to say in 1960 in his previous capacity as Director of the Community Development Services of Manitoba:

> Indian communities, even though they may be located at the very doors of all kinds of job prospects, do not provide the kinds of experience which permit them to make use of job opportunities. . . . They do not develop the kind of personality that fits easily into the work situation. If Community Development cannot bring a group of Indians to a level where they can respond to these conditions in a positive way, it will have failed.

In other words, community development has to be tried in order to see whether it can help Indians ultimately to move away from their reserves with some prospect of economic success. Dr. Sol Tax,[5] speaking at Queen's University, Kingston, in June 1960, suggested that economic projects on the reserves may correspond to the cottage-industry stage of evolution towards industrial society and that the Indian may need to go through this stage. Without the projects and processes associated with community development, he would lack that experience.

In the third place, unless people can obtain by their own efforts the things they want, they cannot create within themselves the spirit of self-respect, pride and self-reliance. To object that community development can do nothing more than bolster the economy of Indian communities by a far-fetched variety of tiny projects not only is somewhat inaccurate but misses the main point. What the Indians need above all is to be able to confront the white man today with a sense of achievement. "Then why don't the Indians leave the reserves *en masse?*", the critic will ask. The answer is that not only would that be disastrous if they tried but that six out of every seven still do not want to leave, and for the following reasons. First, though they resent relief, very many Indians are dependent on it; this subsidizing of their lives—though it is not causing dependency

—is helping to perpetuate a situation of which dependency is a part. Second, the Indians are fearful lest they be hurt by white prejudice and discrimination in the outside world. Third, the cultural background of some Indian groups—so we are told—emphasizes withdrawal from strange contacts and especially withdrawal from what all city dwellers except the submerged one-tenth are engaged in—the drive for high status. If these really are the reasons why most Indians stick to their reserves despite their deep need to register positive achievements, the way to modify the factors is the community development way. The multiplication of even apparently trivial production and service operations on the reserves, the planning of them, the simple training for them, can begin to affect the psychological situation favourably. If some white volunteers—intelligent and sympathetic young people from the cities—can, at least occasionally, be their collaborators in these projects, the hurt to Indian pride that is now so deep can begin to be healed and the sulking suspicion of the white man can be gradually overcome. As for Indian distaste for high status, the community development process is relevant to this. The community development approach, in fact, seems well calculated to respect the sensibilities of Indians while providing them, little by little, with the experience of change and the satisfaction of achievement.

To reject these remarks as being beside the point would be easy. But if we are tempted to do this, might it not be that we misunderstand even our own very different kind of culture? Both E. E. Hagen[6] and D. C. McClelland[7] in the United States have carried out considerable research tending to show that what impels individuals to economic enterprise and the fostering of its development is not, as Karl Marx and capitalist economists alike believe, "the profit motive" but the *achievement motive*. A fine example of a living Indian who expresses this motive to perfection but who, in terms of status and wealth, seems at first sight a poor example is Dr. Gilbert C. Monture. A well-known mining engineer, a United Nations consultant on development problems in many countries of the world, a former senior civil servant in the Canadian federal government, former vice-president of an international industrial concern and a member of the Order of the British Empire, he has expressed himself thus:

I don't care whether I have five dollars in the bank or five thousand. Money for money's sake or for material possession does not mean anything. That is part of the Indian-ness in me. . . . What do *you* struggle for? You work like hell for fifty weeks so that you may have two weeks to go out to do a little fishing and hunting. Well, the Indian does this fifty-two weeks of the year.

Those who have met Gilbert Monture have never doubted that *the desire to achieve* was what led him into a high socio-economic status which for him had no intrinsic interest. By working with white men both in voluntary organizations and in governments, he has overcome "fear of strange contacts".[8] Because of his still close link with the Six Nations Reserve, he is a strong supporter of community development. Since he knows that what is needed is technical knowledge, capital, and individuals eager to innovate, he sees community development as involving other people than those who are members of the community to be developed.

The idea that community development is self-help in the rigorous sense of excluding any other kind of help is simply a legacy of the earliest reactions of groups who had been victims of paternalism. This paternalism can be, and often has been, private. What was even more resented, however, was the paternalism of government. Some time therefore had to elapse before a definition of community development such as has been proposed by the Secretary General of the United Nations could find widespread acceptance: "the processes by which the efforts of the people themselves are united with those of *governmental* authorities to improve the economic, social and cultural conditions of communities, to integrate these communities into the life of the nation, and to enable them to contribute to national progress".

This definition, it is true, lays stress on the primary importance of voluntary action by those who wish to develop themselves. At the same time the definition assigns a definite function to government, on the ground that the government has an interest in this development. This interest is to integrate the people into national life so that they can make their proper contribution.

Although on this view community development may be regarded as both a personal and a social investment, it is above all else a form of continuing education. To the government, the unity and advancement of the nation may be the uppermost aim. To the people on

Indian reserves, it could be that the economic aspect of development is uppermost. But the Churches, and other private bodies, perhaps, are well placed for judging as impartial spectators. As was said in 1960 by the Indian-Eskimo Association:[9]

> . . . our conviction is that only by the present generation of Indians coming to grips with the problems of communities that they can regard as their own will the social-psychological consequences occur that will enable their children to move—with some prospects of success because with some measure of equipment—into other, larger and more "modern" communities. This is the supreme advantage of "community development" on the reserves—that it is *educational*, that by promoting change in activities and in the degree of local responsibility for them it can produce a change in general outlook, in self-reliance and initiative.

Because of the artificial isolation and legal peculiarity of Indians on reserves, they urgently need nowadays suitable social opportunities for re-creating their self-reliance and the spirit of liberty. Unfortunately, for the last century they have been so incapsulated from the surrounding social changes that they have felt no challenge to respond to them and now find themselves almost disqualified from doing so. The consequent apathetic resignation helps to promote their unpopularity with the general public (in striking contrast to the enterprising and ever-smiling Eskimos), and reinforces the socio-economic prejudice they encounter in the predominantly non-Indian areas. Unless the present decade can fructify some of the developments of recent years, a further grave deterioration—in Indian affairs at least—can be expected.

---

[1] There is close similarity between the following account and the "strategy of agricultural development" described by Nicolaas Luykx in *Approaches to Development*, ed. J. D. Montgomery and W. J. Siffin, New York, 1966.

[2] The Canadian Council of Churches might find it an interesting exercise to check whether the processes which led to "Operation Beaver" on the Split Lake Reserve in 1964 resemble those described here.

[3] See Daniel Lerner, *The Passing of Traditional Society* (New York: The Free Press of Glencoe, 1958). He and others have remarked that, when a person becomes aware of another style of life than the one he is used to in his own community, he can imaginatively adopt it, at least experimentally. If he likes it, he can change his own style of life to it.

[4] Jean Lagasse, part author of *The People of Indian Ancestry in Manitoba* (Winnipeg: Department of Agriculture and Immigration, 1959).

[5] Sol Tax is Professor of Anthropology at the University of Chicago.

6 E. E. Hagen, *On the Theory of Social Change: How Economic Growth Begins* (Homewood, Illinois: The Dorsey Press, 1962).

7 D. C. McClelland, *The Achieving Society* (Princeton, N.J.: D. Van Nostrand Co., 1961).

8 There are other aspects of this "withdrawal from strange contacts". (a) Because of the divorce of Indians from other Canadians, the life of the nation has almost certainly been the loser. How much the loser is suggested by the contributions made to the national life by such Indians as the following, who by sheer force of character have brought themselves back into the mainstream: Brigadier Martin, the distinguished Mohawk and magistrate; the Rev. Dr. Peter Kelly, a Haida from the Queen Charlotte Islands who served as Moderator of the B.C. Conference of the United Church a few years before his death; and Dr. Gilbert Monture, O.B.E., from the Six Nations Reserve, who is now connected with the Atlantic Development Board. (b) Whites themselves have withdrawn from "strange contacts" with the Indians; as a result they undervalue Indians; this undervaluing is at the bottom of the prejudice, and sometimes the outright discrimination, the Indians suffer.

9 Brief prepared by the Indian-Eskimo Association of Canada for the Parliamentary Committee on Indian Affairs, Ottawa, March 1960, p. 7.

CHAPTER 13

Community Development:
The Role of the Government

The three most important developments in Indian affairs of recent years have been those about which least can be said since their effects were largely in the psychological field. They were the setting up of the Joint Committee of Senate and the House of Commons for investigating the administration of Indian Affairs and for making recommendations; the development of training programmes for Indian chiefs and councillors in band council management and community leadership; and the institution of training programmes in community development for staff of the Indian Affairs Branch. The first of these dates from 1959, with sittings of the committee occupying also the year 1960; the second dates from 1961; and the third from 1965. It would be a gross exaggeration to say that they have changed the whole atmosphere in which Indian affairs are conducted, either by Indians themselves or by those people (chiefly non-Indians) who provide government services to Indians. But they have modified the attitude considerably; indeed, the training programmes for Indian Affairs Branch staff may yet turn out to be of decisive importance.

This particular development, however, like the training programmes for Indian community leaders, would not have occurred (or would not have occurred so soon) without all that was stirred up by the meetings of the Joint Parliamentary Committee, which itself would not have been born without the embarrassments caused to Prime Minister Diefenbaker by the strongly critical comments on Canadian native affairs policy presented to him during his foreign tour in 1959. The most striking thing, however, about the Parliamentary Committee was neither its origin nor the interest it aroused among the Indians by its proposals for greater provincial government participation in their affairs (especially in welfare and education) but that, for the first time, a national voluntary organization—the Indian-Eskimo Association of Canada, representative of groups of the native peoples and of influential white Canadian groups—was available to make representations to it. An emphasis upon the need for the community development approach, and the implications of this both for a new role for Branch staff and for new responsibilities for Indians themselves were forcefully put forward in the Association's brief. The ensuing training programmes have been consistent with the recommendations.

These training programmes have been provided either by the Indian Affairs Branch on a regional basis or by one or another of the provinces wherever a provincial government has decided to recognize (as Ontario and British Columbia have already done) Indian band councils as responsible "municipalities" for particular purposes—e.g., welfare administration or highways or sanitation. Experience has shown that these programmes are more successful and effective in a practical sense if at least two Indians are brought from each band, so that two sets of opinions and proposals can be taken back to the local Indian community for discussion among the members and for the possible taking of implementive action.

By distinction, the training programmes for (usually *non*-Indian) development specialists within the government service have been organized on a more thoroughgoing plan and with stronger budgetary support than those for Indian voluntary workers. The main programme, national in scope, was initiated two years ago, and comprised forty-one members, half of whom were drawn from the field. Coming from various government jobs (including teaching, nursing, and agriculture) and representing various age groups and the several regions of Canada, they had to meet the not altogether pleasant requirements of facing up to all their assumptions about "the Indians" and all the implications of their non-Indian culture, as well as coming to terms with themselves. The experience was, of course, calculated to improve their attitudes towards Indians—hopefully with a view to diminishing the suspicion and even hostility with which Indians may have been viewing *them*. All the members of the course were university graduates. Since as yet there are very few Indian graduates (and practically none within the government service), the scheme calls for "supplementary" training which, within the three years 1965-68, should increase the number of trained assistant development officers from twenty-five to seventy-five. By greatly extending the opportunities of university education for Indians, it is hoped before the end of this period to attract more Indians of suitable calibre into the development programme. It is also hoped that the government may recoup its investment by withdrawing from the field, or at least to the sidelines, many non-Indian officers whose "custodial" or "protective" presence on or near the reserves or at meetings of band councils is still felt to be necessary.

In view of this project of staff training for development, the establishment of the federal post of Director of Development becomes intelligible. This new director now co-ordinates three great areas of governmental activity—social programmes (including welfare), economic development, and engineering and construction (including housing). Better housing and better social services to the reserves will, it is said, precede the industrial development that the government foresees. But it seems clear that, though capital is still very short for helping to ensure that, economically at least, Indians can better help themselves, the present ceiling on the Indian Loan Fund will be raised as soon as sound ideas for productive growth are sparked by the Indians themselves.

Community development, staff development, and co-ordination of administrative functions are now being complemented by a larger measure of decentralization both from Ottawa to the regions (usually provinces) and from the regions to the localities than has hitherto been attempted. To comment on the last point first: the job of the local superintendent is being construed in new terms. Instead of being bogged down by administrative routine, he is being given the training and opportunity to serve as a facilitator and as a counsellor to the Indians; he is helping to extend the exercise of responsibility by band councils, and is securing to them a less inadequate provision for effective development programmes. At the regional level, greater authority is being given to the regional supervisor (who functions as a general manager) and to his specialist senior staff; the main posts are being filled with more highly qualified persons who work as a team and increasingly develop a working contact with non-governmental (not excluding Indian) organizations. There is now much more effort at in-service training. Finally, at the federal level, greater use is being made of the facilities for mutual consultation between the various government organs whose work relates to, or includes dealing with, Indians. One very important principle, which antedates the administrative and other reforms proposed by the Joint Parliamentary Committee but which has received a strong impetus from them, is that, *wherever feasible*, the federal government should no longer provide—still less create—special services of its own to Indians and instead should use existing services of other agencies, notably provincial governments, on terms of reimbursing or at least sharing their costs. Provided that Indian sentiment on the matter is not disregarded, a most sympathetic and indeed urgent attention should be given to finding the ways to implement this principle. The Indians themselves have some serious doubts whether *all* provincial governments would be equally and adequately dutiful to them. Their fears may not be groundless. If Indians are to be persuaded to give new arrangements a reasonable trial, safeguards will have to be devised to counter their fears. But outside Indian ranks the standard—and valid—objection to the principle in question is that it runs counter to traditional constitutional arrangements.

In Chapter 5 the peculiar constitutional connection of the Indians with the federal government of Canada was spelled out.[1] Outside the province of Newfoundland, only the federal government bears legal responsibility for Indians. Other provinces may *feel* responsible for the well-being of Indians living within their territorial limits; they may, through their governments, discharge certain functions on behalf of these Indians. But they are not obliged so to do. The Act that places the responsibility on the federal government is not a Canadian Act at all but a statute of the Parliament of Westminster—the British North America Act of 1867. When reserves were being set up (chiefly after 1870), the federal government was acting according to its statutory responsibility for "Indians and Indian lands". The B.N.A. Act did not require the setting up of reserves, though their establishment was a possible way in which the federal government could interpret its duties. But today the task is to re-integrate "Indians and Indian lands". This integration could occur in one of two ways. Either the federal government could delegate *administrative* responsibility for Indian affairs to the provincial governments, while remaining legally responsible for securing that this administration safeguarded and promoted the interests of Indians, or the B.N.A. Act could be amended to transfer the legal responsibility from the federal government to the provincial governments (leaving the Territories a federal responsibility). While the second method would on the whole be more satisfactory, there is the difficulty that the Government of Canada cannot itself amend the Act passed at Westminster. But the government of Mr. Lester Pearson did once indicate that it would seek to "repatriate" the B.N.A. Act and, once it was back in Canadian hands, the Canadian Parliament would seek agreement to certain formulas for amending it. We may therefore be nearer one of the solutions for placing the Indians and Indian lands within the jurisdiction of provinces than most of us have been thinking. If it turns out that we are not, then the other solution is still possible. Certainly the time ought long ago to have passed when provincial governments could escape the charge of indifference to Indians by pleading jurisdictional incompetence.

Though some provincial governments are still showing reluctance to assume the job of providing services to Indians,[2] a fair number of joint schemes are already in operation and include, in addition to those previously mentioned, programmes in the areas of wildlife and fisheries, fur conservation, wild-crop harvesting, schooling, and hospital services. There are also some agreements with provincial governments for sharing the costs of specialist development officers serving Indian and Métis communities. Reference may be made at this point to the rather imaginative development that brought the famous Métis novelist Yves Thériault into the post of Commissioner for Indian Arts. The Branch has for years maintained an advisory and marketing service in the various provinces for Indian handcrafts; more recently, the provincial governments of Saskatchewan and Manitoba have themselves entered this field of enterprise. But there was a clear need for a commissioner with a nation-wide responsibility for working with those Indians and Indian groups who are concerned for an Indian cultural renascence and a worthy contribution to Canadian literature, painting, folk song, folklore, and dance.

From the point of view of the Indians, the principal difficulty stemming from exclusive federal jurisdiction over their affairs has been their inability to benefit from the provisions of federal legislation that enjoins or permits joint federal-provincial services. There are now signs that more and more breaches will be made in the wall separating Indians from services available through this type of legislation.[3] The two most striking examples are provided by the use that may be made, on behalf of Indians and Indian communities, of the Technical and Vocational Training Assistance Act and the Agricultural Rehabilitation and Development Act of 1961.

The first of these two Acts provides greatly increased federal grant-aid to the provinces to help them train both youths and adults for skilled employments. The Technical and Vocational Training Agreement under the Act offers nine programmes, of which the fifth—Program for the Training of the Unemployed—is the one within which it has been found possible to include a fair number of unemployed Indians, especially youths. Owing to the low scholastic level of most Indians, Program 5 often has to be supplemented by school grade courses to bring the trainees up to the minimum level at which training can effectively begin. It should be noted that, under this programme, training may be of a refresher type, and not simply for an occupation not previously followed by the trainee.

As for the A.R.D.A. programme, this was set up as a result of a Senate Committee on land use in the rural areas. The basic ideas behind this programme are that, if there is to be an effective attack on the problem of poverty in the rural areas, human beings are one of the resources needing development and that in any case the problems of the rural areas cannot be entirely solved in the rural sector. Over Canadian society as a whole, there are rapidly changing requirements for manpower, and this fact points to the need for more adequate information about these requirements and more adequate training to meet them, in the countryside as well as elsewhere. Consistently with this, each province has now set up a joint federal-provincial A.R.D.A. Committee and, by reform in the administration of the scheme for the current quinquennium (1965-70), each committee, instead of waiting for decisions upon its proposals from the federal government, may proceed to implement its projects.[4] It is now foreseen that "Indians and Indian lands" will be included within the scheme whenever a particular province so desires and whenever a satisfactory basis for this inclusion can be worked out. The A.R.D.A. Committee of Saskatchewan has already adopted a project within which Indian communities are incorporated. It may be added that, since the A.R.D.A. programme is, in effect, concerned with other primary industries as well as agriculture, some attention, especially in the Northland, is now being given to ways in which the native peoples—Eskimos as well as Indians—

may be trained for mining employment. Already there have been Indian and Eskimo training courses to develop skills in mining, prospecting, and the petroleum industry, and the matter of better use of these peoples' manpower resources has been officially canvassed in a Ministry of Mines Conference held fairly recently in Victoria. Both of the major enactments mentioned above and the activities arising from them now seem likely to command greater financial resources and to be more strongly supplemented by related projects and services. Canada now seems more aware—perhaps as a consequence of President Lyndon Johnson's "War on Poverty"— of the physical and human under-development within its own borders. Hence the government of Mr. Lester Pearson announced in the 1965 Throne Speech its intention of building up social and economic opportunity. Shortly afterwards, the government set up a "Special Program Committee of the Cabinet", under the chairmanship of the Prime Minister, to develop new policies and programmes for alleviating poverty. To assist the Committee, a Special Planning Secretariat was established. Working through government departments and agencies (including private agencies outside government), the Secretariat plans and co-ordinates the attack on a front that is wider than the merely economic. For example, Medicare will be established next year and used as one weapon against under-development. Legislation in 1965 established the Company of Young Canadians—counterpart of the U.S. Peace Corps except that, unlike the Corps and indeed C.U.S.O. (Canadian Universities Service Overseas), it will concentrate on working with underprivileged people *within* the nation. In the strictly economic sector, there will be grants and loans to unemployed workers moving to fresh employment,[5] new measures of assistance to the "special" or "depressed" areas,[6] and increased federal aid to the work of A.R.D.A. committees for retraining workers and for broadening the economic base of rural communities. Finally, the federal government has announced its intention of introducing legislation for a fifty-fifty cost-sharing Canada Assistance Plan, whose details will take account of the point of view of the provinces but whose basic principle will be a federal contribution to the cost of assisting needy applicants on a basis of need rather than an income test.

All these anti-poverty and service programmes are of great interest to the Indian and Eskimo population. Not the least important are the three not directly related to industrial training and development. First, Medicare. Though the (erstwhile) Indian and Northern Health Service Branch of the Department of National Health and Welfare had made stupendous progress, especially since 1944, in rooting out T.B. among the native peoples and in securing provision of preventive and other health programmes in very difficult circumstances and at extremely high per-capita cost, the federal government had always made clear to the Indian and Eskimo users that programmes were not available as of right even though, until a few years ago, they were virtually free. The latter-day development of provincial Hospital Insurance Commissions has meant, however, that Indian band members, using their facilities, are now being encouraged to take out group insurance schemes through their band councils. In effect, they are beginning to pay for what formerly, as a result of their acute poverty, they had received as an act of grace. Since Indian per-capita income is only one-sixth of the average income of other Canadians and since in real terms the discrepancy is probably as great for Eskimos too, a "health service crisis" would have been rapidly approaching for them unless Medicare had come along to head it off. For, while Medicare will be a contributory scheme, it will also be available to those who for one reason or another cannot contribute to it. Second, the projects of the Company of Young Canadians will, it is hoped, be a contributory scheme in a different sense, whereby the Indian or Eskimo can contribute to the development of his own community alongside the volunteer from outside. Collaboration, in this very literal meaning, may well do much to increase mutual knowledge, respect and friendliness between the original and the more recent settlers in Canada, aside altogether from any material benefit accruing from the co-operative effort. It will also indicate particular ways in which the native peoples may help themselves better without the backing of large capital resources. Third, the Canada Assistance Plan, if it can be extended to apply to the native peoples, may help overcome difficulties in one of the most contentious programmes—the welfare handouts—which the Indian Affairs Branch and the Northern Administration Branch have been required to administer. For, rightly or wrongly, the native peoples have continued to harbour resentment based on the belief that, under present arrangements, they are less eligible for welfare than are other Canadians.

The Canadian "War on Poverty" has already raised the question: "What is poverty?" Mr. Maurice Sauvé, a Minister in the present Pearson administration, has said that it is "a condition in which people are for any reason prevented from enjoying certain minimum advantages or benefits afforded by the level of civilization in Canada today." If that is so, then it is a condition over which Indians and Eskimos have only a minimal amount of control. A more penetrating definition has been offered by Dr. Albert Rose of the University of Toronto School of Social Work in the statement that "Poverty . . . is not merely a matter of income. It may be and very often is a 'state of mind'. If I were asked to decide whether one family or another were 'poor', I would want to know not merely their income and assets but their hopes and aspirations for themselves and their children and the reality of these as related to their educational qualifications, their position and experience in the labour market, their ages and the state of their health."[7] On this basis, the great majority of Indians and Eskimos are very poor. The factors of age and state of health will, it is hoped, be taken account of by Medicare and the Canada Assistance Plan. But there are other factors also relating to employability, and there is little relation between these and Indian-Eskimo "hopes and aspirations" for income. For example, according to figures given in Chapter 6, while over 57,000 Indians were at school, fewer than 100 were at university,[8] only 1,000 were taking vocational courses, and fewer than 4,000 were in high school. As for the material poverty of which some details were given in Chapter 8, the following statistics should be added, first, for Indians in the provinces and, later, for Eskimos and Indians in the North.

(a) Out of every 1,000 live Indian births in the provinces, 74.7 (against 27.2 for the whole of Canada) will not survive. (b) Fifty-seven per cent of all Indian families occupy sub-standard houses or shacks of three rooms or less, without electricity. (c) Only 11 per cent of Indian homes have sewerage, indoor lavatories, and baths (sewers or septic tanks, 9 per cent; running water, 13 per cent; indoor lavatories, 9 per cent; baths, 7 per cent). (d) Thirty thousand families occupy twenty-six thousand houses. (e) Unemployment is eight to ten times the national average. (f) Seventy-five per cent of Indian families earn less than $2,000 a year. (g) Thirty-six per cent of Indian families need welfare assistance each year.

Statistics for Eskimos and Indians in the Northwest Territories are as follows: (a) In 1961, Indians and Eskimos together accounted for 57.5 per cent of the population;[9] the rest of the population consisted of whites. The average wage in that year was $4,460 for males and $2,425 for females. But while there were 741 whites earning $4,000 to $4,999 (males and females combined), there were only one hundred native inhabitants (Eskimos and Indians of both sexes) in that earning bracket.[10] (b) For two years, it was estimated that 47.1 per cent of Indian males and 40.9 per cent of Eskimo males had average annual earnings of less than $2,000, as against only 8.9 per cent among the whites.[11] If these statistics seem to show that northern Indians—*a fortiori* the Eskimos—are doing much better than the southern Indians resident in the provinces, it should be borne in mind that general costs are from 50 to 75 per cent higher in the North. (c) A further insight into northern living standards is provided by the statistic that, although the national infant mortality rate is less than one in thirty, one in every four Eskimo children dies before the age of twelve months.

The biggest single reason for the very high infant mortality rate (as well as much ill health) is the very poor housing. Attributable to the same factor is the low scholastic achievement of the school children who, for their homework, lack privacy, decent light, and often tables and chairs and other relevant aids such as parental encouragement. As a result, more and more of the native people are becoming thoroughly restive about their home conditions and uneasy when, through lack of running water, they cannot "keep clean and tidy on an equal footing"[12] with others. Much sound argument could be advanced for the view that one way to break the spiral of poverty would be through an imaginative programme of decent public housing.[13] As at present, substantial contributions, individually or collectively made, of land, labour and building materials would be expected of the Eskimos and Indians themselves, not only as users of the houses but for creating an equity-interest or reducing total costs and stimulating a pride in ownership.

Towards these ends, the then Minister of Citizenship and Immigration, who in the fall of 1965 was also the Director General of Indian Affairs, announced that he was seeking approval for an increased expenditure on housing of $2 million for 1966. Shortly afterwards, the Minister of Northern Affairs, who is *now* the Director General of Indian Affairs, promised $12 million over five years and a further annual "subsidy" of $2 million for Eskimo housing.[14] Our national housing authority, the Central Mortgage and Housing Corporation, has, in former years, been rather inflexible in the standards (as distinct from the type) of housing it will recognize for the purposes of loans to local housing authorities. This standard of house is well outside the pockets of nearly all Indians and Eskimos. Equally, Eskimo community councils and Indian band councils are not recognized by the C.M.H.C. as public housing agencies; hence, these councils are ineligible for housing loans. Only in northern Saskatchewan has any C.M.H.C. money reached the native people for housing purposes, and that loan was underwritten by a co-operative organization.

In the area of social services the situation is just as unsatisfactory, except that in a few provinces arrangements have been made through the Indian Affairs Branch for the provision of child-care services to the reserves by children's aid societies. A few trained social workers are attached both to the Indian Affairs and the Northern Administration Branches, but almost everywhere officials quite untrained for social work operations—Mounted Police officers, Hudson's Bay Company factors, ordinary administrators of the Branches—are having to try to cope with delinquency; corrections; rehabilitation; issue of relief; helping people straighten out the problems arising in families separated by illness, death or other circumstances; adoptions; care of children in transit homes and so forth. The prospects for improvement in this whole area depend largely upon strengthening provincial and territorial responsibilities towards the Indians—responsibilities which these authorities cannot yet discharge very adequately even for non-Indians.

Under the terms of the Technical and Vocational Training Assistance Act, only one programme, it should be recalled, is being made much use of for the native people. The chief importance of Program 5 (despite the useful start it has given to the training of unemployed Indian and Métis youth) still lies in its offering a precedent for the inclusion of persons of Indian ancestry in the other programmes. May this precedent at least be safe!

Concerning industrial development on the reserves, all that can be said has been said already. National fiscal and monetary policy is a responsibility of the federal government; but outside this field, economic planning and development functions belong to the provincial governments which, however, as previously stated, have no constitutional jurisdiction over Indians. On the other hand, the agreements that brought provincial governments into partnership with the federal Indian Affairs Branch in such *ad hoc* programmes as wild-crop harvesting and fur conservation have now been extended to allow for provincial exercise of economic planning and development functions over Indian reserves, whose well-being is inextricably connected with that of the surrounding territory. In Ontario, Manitoba and Saskatchewan these functions are now being exercised. But noteworthy results are not yet forthcoming, and unless A.R.D.A. Committees come to the rescue—with the Indian Affairs Branch contracting with the Committees to provide money from its own budget—the question will still need to be asked: Where is the capital to come from to assist a major economic development on the reserves?

In the Arctic, fortunately, things are not quite so backward. Since 1959 the Eskimos have benefited from an ordinance of the Northwest Territorial Council which set up a Co-operative Section inside the Industrial Division of the Northern Administration Branch. The Branch itself has given powerful support to the establishment of Eskimo co-operatives. Adequate resources from the Eskimo Revolving Loan Fund have been provided to enable these co-operatives to get started; advice on organization and, where relevant, on the marketing of goods in southern Canada and abroad have been made regularly available. But the co-operatives are required to become independent of the government quite quickly and to run their affairs with full responsibility. This they have managed, and they are now actively and successfully engaged in making and selling carvings, sculpture, graphic arts and handicrafts, clothing, footwear and bread. In addition, there are retail stores and, most important of all, Arctic char fisheries.

The rather impressive performance of the Eskimo co-operatives in the last few years and the close identity that can be observed to exist between the membership of co-operative directing boards and of the local Eskimo community councils suggest that if the Eskimos were given a greater measure of self-government, they would rise to the occasion.[15] Except for those of Indian background outside the reserve system, the same thing could not so confidently be said of the Indian population, since this system—as we have shown—has reinforced dependency, stifled initiative, and bred an apathy that will be immensely difficult to dispel. Nevertheless, there is no cure for irresponsibility except stronger and stronger doses of responsibility. As the government clearly sees, the Indian band councils too must be more and more trusted to respond effectively to the challenges of their situation. The probability, however, is that solutions will come piecemeal and by cultural imitation. Further, the movement of change which, for the white settlers and immigrants, has been from east to west may now, for the native peoples, be from north to south.

An important conclusion to which we came after analysing the historical background of Canadian native affairs was that a uniform official policy for Indians and Eskimos is not at present feasible. Though programmes must increasingly be directed towards integrating all the native groups within the nation, and towards making available to them the general services that other Canadians receive, some special permissive services must meanwhile be provided and some of these should be special to particular groups of the native people at some particular time. For instance, the same financial arrangements for developing producer and consumer co-operatives as have succeeded with the Eskimos (and Métis) may not, at this moment, be reproduced with equal success among the Indians. A series of economic, political and social changes that eroded the Indian's place in his own country and that led white settlers to place him where he was disabled from changing himself probably now requires that the Indian should take up the opportunities for change rather more cautiously than did the Eskimos. Two points need to be stressed. Politically, the Indians are powerless; economically, they are not indispensable. Though twenty times as numerous as the Eskimos, they are much more widely dispersed and nowhere form—as the Eskimos in the Northwest Territories form—a large minority within a political division of the country. Hence, while Eskimos constitute a vital component of the membership of the N.W.T. Council, Indians are almost negligible in other assemblies of the nation. Again, while Eskimos are going to be desperately needed to man the prospective industrial developments in the Arctic (since no other economic agents would be so effective in such an environment), the Indians could almost be done without, remaining on the sidelines without serious damage to anyone but themselves.

This is what is perilous in Canadian native affairs—that the Indians may remain quite peripheral to the interests and preoccupations of almost all Canadians and, in a sense, become expendable. Fortunately, there was a very strong statement of policy, on September 18, 1958, by the then Deputy Minister of Northern Affairs and Commissioner of the Northwest Territories, Mr. Gordon Robertson; and his policy appears to have strongly marked both the Diefenbaker and Pearson administrations in their activity north of the sixtieth latitude:

> It is clear that government, in its role under our philosophy, not only provides the basic services expected of government, such as health, education, law and order and necessary administrative and regulatory services, but in a number of other important ways can do much to provide the basis for the industry and finance that can then carry forward with resource development. . . . I should like to add, however, . . . that, in relation to northern development, the federal government has a special and inescapable responsibility to one particular sector of the Canadian public—the native peoples of the north. The standard of living of the northern Indians and of our Canadian Eskimos is far below the national average—indeed below what is regarded as poverty anywhere else. . . . The obligation of government . . . is clear and inescapable. For it, the immediate human problem must never be subordinated to the requirements of physical resource development.

Because these have not proved mere words, there is promise that what has been so well begun among the native peoples of the Arctic may spread to those of the south, helping to liberate and revitalize the Indian communities there and beginning the long, slow process of eroding an unfriendly public's prevalent neglect.

---

[1] See pp. 33-4.

[2] Partly because of disputes between the provincial and federal governments about jurisdiction (i.e., which of the two governments is responsible for action), and partly because of disagreements concerning the amount of reimbursement by the federal government if provincial governments undertake

the provision of services by delegation. While these disputes are not irrational, the delays in providing services can often be inhuman. If Indians are living off the reserve, for instance, and are being deprived of proper housing, sanitation, health measures, schooling for their children and vocational training—as not infrequently happens—the public have a right bluntly to tell both levels of government that they are *jointly* responsible.

3 One of the strongest arguments in the past against Indians' participating in the advantages of federal-provincial legislation, which uses the device of cost-sharing, is that Indians—as a privilege of their status—have been exempt from federal tax on income earned on reserves. They have been exempt also from provincial taxes (including in one or two instances provincial income taxes) because they were resident within enclaves of territory not subject to provincial jurisdiction. These old arguments are breaking down as large numbers of Indians leave their reserves for at least a portion of each year to earn wages from casual or seasonal employment and as they buy from business enterprises in the towns and cities goods such as cigarettes and tobacco, gasoline, textiles and many non-food items subject to excise or sales taxes. Further, provincial governments may and do tax reserve lands (which are federal crown lands) if the lands are being used not by the Indians themselves or by the federal government but, as is not infrequently the case, by non-Indians operating on leases.

4 Provincial Ministers of National Resources form a national council at whose gatherings they meet the appropriate federal Minister (now renamed the Minister of Rural Development and Forestry). Here, projects of resource development are discussed and may become—through the provincial A.R.D.A. Committees—objects of federal assistance by the Department of Finance. Where no provincial governments exist, as in the Territories, a minister of the federal government, e.g. of Northern Affairs, may himself take the initiative in proposing to the Minister of Rural Development and Forestry a project of resource development for grant aid.

5 This programme will be administered by the Canada Manpower Centre of the Ministry of Labour.

6 This programme will be administered by the Minister of Industry.

7 Dr. Albert Rose, School of Social Work, University of Toronto, in an address given on February 19, 1964, to the Association of Women Electors of Toronto and the Social Planning Council of Toronto.

8 Including one Eskimo—the first ever to reach university. Though the Government hopes to have every Eskimo child in school by 1970, 45 per cent of the Eskimo school age population were outside the classroom in 1960-61, while in 1961-62 more than half of the school children in the Northwest Territories were enrolled in the first three grades.

9 The Eskimo number around 10,000.

10 *Canadian Census* (Ottawa, 1961).

11 A. Baliczi, *Vunta Kutchin Social Change* (Ottawa: Northern Coordination and Research Centre, Department of Northern Affairs, 1963).

12 Chief Omer Peters, Union of Ontario Indians, in the *Indian-Eskimo Association Bulletin*, Vol. 6, No. 4, Sept. 1965.

13 A federal programme has recently been announced that will provide, over the next five years, for the building of 12,000 houses ($75 million), for the development of hydro, water and sewage facilities ($24 million), and for new roads on reserves ($10 million). This is by far the biggest programme of material aid so far made available—and very good news indeed.

14 Under this programme 1,560 new houses for Eskimos are to be built.

15 The Carrothers Commission, which visited the Arctic settlements in 1965, is well aware of this.

CHAPTER 14

Community Development:
The Role of the Church

It all used to seem so simple to the simple-minded. The Indians were "a vanishing race". Until they vanished the State would provide custodial protection and "perpetual annuities" for them on the reserves while the Church would provide the cure of souls.

And now things are so complex that the account given in this book is a gross over-simplification.

In this complex situation is there anything that the Church can do and ought to try to do other than what even the simple-minded have always supposed the Church would do?

To begin with, are there any things that the Church must not do?

First, the Churches must not use private gifts as an instrument of inter-Church competition. Perhaps the most serious charge levelled against the Churches has been that, whatever their "calculated reluctance" to distribute relief supplies, they have shown themselves as interested in winning and keeping the "bodies" of our native peoples as in "saving" their souls. A way to dispose of this allegation is to follow a policy (for instance, a community development policy) that clearly contradicts it without ceasing to be humane.[1] Another way is to manifest the ecumenical spirit even if this means negative action of the kind that kept the United Church of Canada out of the Arctic mission field.

Second, the Churches must avoid the accusation of being hypocrites in the matter of property. The idea of property is familiar in the field of human rights. The Churches have inherited certain views on property, as for example the extreme dangers to human personality of an individual's owning too much or too little. Our Indians have, for the most part, an incomplete understanding of private property, though their impression is that the cultural majority in Canada regard it as the supreme good. Where do the

Churches stand on this matter *today?* How does their stand on this matter relate to policy for the native peoples? What about co-operative property? What does the Church make of sharing things? Many Indians are bemused about the answers that would be given by the Churches to these and related questions.

Third, the Churches must not automatically support the "upper crust" of society in that increasing number of northern settlements where, because of immigration from the south, the population is now mixed. In the Arctic, we find the social components of the settlement population to be whites and Eskimos or (in certain localities) whites, Eskimos and Indians. In the northerly parts of most of our provinces, the social components are whites, Métis and Indians. These components are arranged as social layers—the whites being invariably at the top and either Eskimos or Indians at the bottom. Hence, a kind of caste system develops. The whites will consist of the provincial (or federal) government administrator—a sort of general manager; other specialist government officers, federal and provincial (or territorial), such as those occupied in transport, welfare, health, and education; a minister and/or priest; a storekeeper or two; and the manager of the fish-packing station or the mine—with one or two subordinates, clerks and assistants. At the base of the social pyramid will be, say, the Indians, and between the Indians and the whites will be, say, the Métis. Those Métis who are close to the white élite group in their aspirations and style of living will be looked down upon by the whites. Corresponding to the three social layers there will be three informal communications systems. But the rudimentary local government of the area will be inadequate to unite the three layers and instead will become a preserve of the white élite. The economic interests of the whites being as different from those of the other groups as their social status, the machinery of local government will be exploited in their favour and perhaps against the wishes of the higher levels of government. In these circumstances, a tremendous responsibility falls upon the local priest and minister, for they are the only members of the community who, strictly speaking, are without a vested interest or who are not tied by directives from other agencies. Indeed, as has been said,[2] "the Church is the only local voluntary organization which could involve the whole community", and for this reason the professional representatives of the Church occupy a more strategic situation than even the government administrator or co-ordinator. On the personalities of these representatives, on their attitudes and choices, depend the conceptions that the people of native background will form. If they automatically determine these choices by reference to their position as members of the élite, they will confirm native mistrust of the white man and help reinforce paternalism and dependency. The choices they make should not only be rational, they should be Christian.

In turning to consider what the Churches can and must try to do, we should begin by noting that they still command in Canada a vast prestige. Partly this prestige stems from a general belief that the Churches are not (or are no longer) in the government's pocket. In the 1820's and 1830's the suspicion was that the Anglican Church and the Government of Upper Canada were in close league; at that time this suspicion did not help the Anglican Church. And when nowadays, outside Canada, an Archbishop proclaims that the Church's teaching is not opposed to "the idea of a state composed of a number of national or racial groups maintained in their separate and distinct identity", he again is not helping his Church. We look for his address and at least suspect that this "insight" has to do not so much with Christ as with the Archbishop's country of residence.[3]

If the Churches in Canada, however, enjoy a prestige that partly at least comes from their independence, they should use that prestige and the accompanying power for purposes wider than those conventionally thought to be religious. When the Archbishop said what he did, the offence was not that he was making a political judgment but that he was not making a *Christian* judgment. Religion and politics are intertwined as, for instance, politics and economics are intertwined. There is nothing to dismay us in that: the power that used to be organized in types—social, economic, political, religious —is now much more mixed in its character. A business firm exists to do business, but its influence is also social and may be political (its contributions policy will even see to that). Civil services were set up to administer, but their influence and action are nowadays such that they help make the laws and dispense justice. The same kind of general point holds good for the Church. We no longer segregate influence and power according to its kind, even though this influence and power may be recognizably religious rather than economic or political. Again, we no longer centralize this power and influence; we extend it from thrones to parish pulpits and from the clergy to lay men and women. Nowadays not only are types of power mixed but the power itself is widely diffused.

This is highly convenient. If we truly believe that religion should find its way into every nook and cranny of life, then the multiple reference of a power recognizably religious is a very good thing. And if we truly believe that the Church is not the clergy alone but ordinary members of the Church also, then the democratizing of the Church is a very good thing as well. So long as religious influence was restricted to the walls of church buildings, critics could always allege that this influence was irrelevant to the outside world where other influences had their natural play. And so long as ecclesiastical power was confined to ordained persons, critics could claim that this ordained group was an élite whose standards did not hold for the mass of mankind. But the changes now occurring in Church power and influence are beginning to cut the ground from beneath the critics' feet. The Church is now becoming part of "the target system". It wants to change persons; it wants a new system of interpersonal relationships. How can the Church relate itself to the system it hopes to create? And the answer is: by itself *being* that system.

We are fond of talking of systems. And the plain fact is that we must continue to talk of them and must return to talk of them almost at once. But the Church is essentially concerned with persons. These people have their personal needs; they have their own private and family lives to live. This is particularly true of those who do not go out to work but have to spend their lives in the home.

Priests, ministers and ministers' wives working among our native people have to be down-to-earth. How can Mrs. A. be helped to budget her money—does she really know what budgeting is? And what about the possibilities of a potato patch, a kitchen garden? Does Mrs. B. know where she can best buy sewing thread for her machine? Why not let Mrs. C. know some new methods of child care, and Mrs. D. something about balanced diets? William Wordsworth spoke about the "little nameless, unremembered acts". These have a great part to play in improving life for people and, to return to the earlier point, in building a new system of interpersonal relationships.

We have already said that part of the Church's prestige comes from its independence. The Church's role in fact is that of a mediator—a duly constituted society placed between the government and the people, serving as a spiritual bond between them and influencing all. It is not only that the Church is the bearer of a culture higher than any that has so far been achieved in secular society; it is that the Church seeks to express this other culture in its internal and external relationships.[4] For this reason the Church is well fitted to help our native people to bridge the gap between a less developed and a more developed way of life.

The Church, however, is very seriously hindered in this task by current white prejudice against Indians and even by outright discrimination. To some extent, of course, these white attitudes are an indication of the Church's own failure with some of its own members. They indicate also a measure of failure to bring a moral and spiritual impact to bear on the lives of the ordinary citizens. Therefore, they indicate, finally, a measure of failure in shaping the values which—as we said in Chapter 1—government itself should represent in a representative democracy. The equality of all its citizens and their equal rights to be treated as citizens are elementary points of justice in democratic society. The Church ought not, however, to be hampered in its own work by the government's weakness in this regard.

The greatest of all the values we can expect of secular government is justice; it is therefore in relation to this value that the Church should be most active and uncompromising. "I feel bitter when a next-door neighbour tells me, 'It is our Company's policy not to hire Indians to work in our northern plant,'" confesses an Indian woman living in an Ontario town.[5] ". . . The General Manager of one of northern Manitoba's largest mines declared that he would not have an Indian in his plant, his hospital or on his street," reported a United Church minister.[6] "Remember, bring no more Indians to this city," said a Toronto businessman to me in 1962, although I was accompanied to the interview by an Indian colleague newly arrived from the Northwest Territories. "And if the Indians are really starving in Manitoba," I overheard a young white man say to his two friends in the subway, "why the devil don't they eat their dogs?"

In these ways we deeply insult the culture, the pride, and the dignity of these people. We must remind ourselves that in those parts of the "Christian" world where these insults have been institutionalized and systematized through "racial groups maintained in their separate and distinct identity", our white civilization is beginning to be repudiated. Men who happen to be white are being mistrusted or treated as inferior, for no other reason than that they are white. The traditional demand by Christianity for acceptance of people of different culture or racial background is being increasingly replaced by a demand by yellow, brown and black men for their *total separation*. This is a fact that most whites—because of their unbelievably arrogant assumption of superiority—cannot even yet take in. They cannot believe that any Chinese or Canadian Indians or American Negroes or South African Bantus will regard whites as inferior to themselves or that any of them will prefer the way of segregation. Yet the truth is that, after long years of ignominy and nonentity, the unaccepted people, or many of them, do not wish any longer to be "tainted" and "corrupted" by contact with whites.

The person whom *Maclean's* magazine has called "the beautiful segregationist", our own Canadian Indian Miss Kahn-Tineta Horn of Caughnawaga in Quebec, has emphasized that this is the ground of her own opposition to integration. Even when Indians reject Miss Horn's anti-integration policies, they have to justify to themselves their own fear and mistrust of white men—from those in the government downwards—by invoking the evidence of history and rhetorically asking whether they have not good reason for fear and mistrust. The Churches have a truly staggering task in restoring the confidence of Indians, and perhaps of Eskimos too. All the more reason, therefore, for making social justice the central value in its mission of reconciliation.

Winning the confidence of Indians and Eskimos is not a matter of assuming that they are always right and everyone else always wrong. It is a matter of helping them to help themselves better— a cliché that sums up the whole truth. By reason of their relatively small numbers, their linguistic difficulties and their lack of organizational resources and techniques, the native peoples cannot yet adequately plead their own cause. Although they are beginning to know how—as is evidenced by newspaper coverage for the National Brotherhood of British Columbia and the National Indian Council— someone meanwhile has to help them to do it. The Churches, which maintain ministers, priests and teachers in so many Indian and Eskimo communities, are the obvious agencies

1. to inform their own members concerning the broad situation of Indians and Eskimos;
2. to defend the cause of Indians and Eskimos within the nation;[7]
3. to criticize the inadequacies of public policies;
4. to propose changes in policies and new or broadened Indian-Eskimo programmes.

To perform these tasks adequately, the Churches will need on certain occasions to join forces and on other occasions to act on their own. But they will be acting most effectively and best helping the native peoples to help themselves if they will give every possible support, short of interference, to native efforts to build and maintain their own organizations. The Churches have done a magnificent job of this kind in some of the larger cities of the country: it needs now to be extended to the rural areas. The Churches must not look for any returns on their investment in this business: indeed, their participation in these new institutions of the native peoples ought to be through dedicated Church members drawn from the ranks of these peoples. In this way they will be bringing the desired national influence to bear through what we previously called a moral and spiritual impact on the lives of ordinary citizens. This has the advantage of fostering the sense of self-responsibility among the native peoples and a sense that they are working for social justice as free men.

Among these peoples, social justice seems roughly to mean what the English, in metaphors drawn from sport, call "fair play" and "playing the game". It is unlikely that Indians will want the same kinds of things or at least the same quantities of the same kinds of things as seem to make most non-Indians happy (or keep them unhappy). But Indians will want to be treated, socially and politically, as equals and to be respected for what they are (all their real differences from the rest of us being included). And they will want to escape from economic aimlessness and to have both a sense of purpose and an ultimate pride in achievement. Finally, they will want, as the reward of labour, a decent shelter, good if simple food, adequate clothing, medical care, and an opportunity for their children to develop their full educational potential.

It ought not to be beyond the capacity of Canadian society, when linked to Indian capacity and resolution, to contrive that Indians achieve social justice in this sense. We ought to count ourselves lucky that Indians would feel society had "played the game" by them in securing to them those modest expectations. No immigrant groups would be so easily pleased, for non-Indians tend to view justice in mathematical terms: "If 10 per cent more for you, then 10 per cent more for me." The Indian would forget to ask—or rather would not think of asking—whether someone else was doing better than he, provided he had enough. The trouble so far in the twentieth century has been that the Indian has certainly not had enough.

One way of helping him towards obtaining by his own efforts a little more than he now has, and therefore one way of working for social justice, is through community development. The Churches should be the staunchest advocates of community development. It may be true, as some people have urged, that community development, by enforcing the need for permanent residence, may somewhat diminish the Indian's income that at present accrues from a semi-nomadic way of life; if true, the loss would not only be trivial, it would be short-term. The long-term purpose of community development is not to be reckoned in material terms at all, though in terms still relevant to social justice.

The strategy of community development includes accustoming the native people to a wider view of Christian missions, of private organizations, and government authority. It therefore provides further opportunities for overcoming the gap between the native people and other Canadians, eliminating or at least reducing their fear and suspicion.

As we mentioned once before, the natural response by those who have suffered a colonialist attitude is to try to eliminate all traces of it even if this means cutting off their nose to spite their face. There are none so orthodox as the newly converted. Yet, again as we have seen, government is *not* irrelevant to local development enterprise. Nor are voluntary organizations, including the Churches. The definition quoted previously from the United Nations Secretary General clearly implied that mutual aid is what we need. Not the Indian or the Eskimo "going it alone"; still less, the government or volunteers doing the whole job; but the native people, the volunteer forces, and statutory authority uniting their contributions under the lead of those whose development needs are to be met. No Indian has need to fear, when whites come from outside—as officers or as volunteers—to unite their resources with those of people inside, that community development is thereby condemned to dilution or erosion. The spirit of this development remains so long as government and others who are in a helping role impose nothing on the people and probe always for the people's own ideas. Most important of all, when community development occurs in this spirit, the native people will recognize the spirit of fair play—with favourable effects for their own attitudes towards the non-Indian partners.[8] As someone has said, attitudes do not exist in the abstract. They are always a response to situations. The traditional Indian attitude to the white man was such a response; community development can change both the situation and the response.

If "we are all members one of another", it makes sense to argue that Canada as a whole suffers (primarily, in a spiritual way) when so many of the inhabitants of its native communities remain impoverished. Their hardship is one not of simple poverty but of a certain kind of poverty. As we all know, there is decent poverty and demoralizing poverty. Too much of the poverty among our native peoples is the latter kind—a misery whose constituent features of despair and strong drink act upon each other and compound the wretchedness. It is a wretchedness that can turn into delinquency and crime—the wretchedness of apathy, of having nothing left to stir curiosity or passion. Poverty such as this will not be removed by the welfare state alone. Statutory authority needs help from the private agency; the public body requires aid from the voluntary organization; government and Church must co-operate as partners. And so, while it makes sense to prescribe distinctive roles for government and Church, it also makes sense to say that more important still is that the sum of their influence and power be well distributed through society.

If this could be achieved, a more positive form of response to social issues would occur. Too often we praise our permissive society for being ready to offer support if formally requested. But, in the sacred names of self-determination and democratic non-intervention, are we content to be simply a *potential* alliance for a *potential* progress? Or is our understanding of human beings deep enough, our concern for them serious enough, and are our principles flexible yet firm enough, for us to be able to see what we must do and where it would be dilatoriness (not patience), neglect (not respect for others), indifference (not respect for their freedom) if we did not unite our forces and powerfully move in?

The British Prime Minister, speaking in Montreal on February 28, 1964, said that the world had fifteen years to prove that the "split of humanity" between the whites and the coloured peoples would be closed. Otherwise, he added, "a fissure will have been created, a lack of trust, a gap of understanding, which no subsequent efforts will be able to mend: there comes a time when the past so dominates the pattern of the future that all the goodwill in the world will not change the course that has been set." These words cannot any longer be construed as a dire warning to us in Canada that the "split of humanity" is irremediable. But the words can remind us to keep that sense of times and seasons and that continuing enthusiasm of humanity that belong to the role of the Church in society.

---

1 V. F. Valentine, in his *The Métis of Saskatchewan* (1955), has identified some incipient phases of inter-Church conflicts which often consume leadership energies and divert attention from community development.

2 Dr. W. B. Baker, *Community Development in Northern Saskatchewan*, unpublished paper, 1960.

3 The quotation (February 18, 1964) is from the Most Reverend William Patrick Whelan, Roman Catholic Archbishop of Bloemfontein, Union of South Africa.

4 Bishop Gore in *Christ and Society* (London: Allen and Unwin, 1928) writes: "the pagan Caecilius, in the dialogue of Minucius Felix, though he speaks of the Christians with the utmost contempt and bitterness, yet is represented as saying: 'They manage to recognize each other . . . loving each other almost before they are acquainted.'" But St. Luke (as well as St. Matthew) represents Jesus as extending the obligation of brotherly love to all: 'What credit is it if you love [only] those who love you?'"

5 See *Thunderbird*, May 1964 (Winnipeg: National Indian Council).

6 See Rev. Chas. R. Catto, in *Breaking the Barriers* (Toronto: United Church of Canada, 1964), p. 92.

7 For instance, Indians and Eskimos are often innocently blamed, even by well-wishers, for not pulling their weight more. It is assumed that the native peoples are lapsing into a greater and greater lethargy. In fact, this is untrue, and it would serve their cause if it were known to be so.

8 P. T. Bauer and B. S. Yamey in their *Economics of Under-developed Countries* (Nisbet and Cambridge University Press, 1957) have argued against some of the forms of government aid to under-developed people which we ourselves might unhesitatingly support. Their argument is the reasonable one

that "those who make erroneous decisions [must] suffer losses". They obviously fear that community development may be construed as a system in which the State always pays the piper though it never calls the tune and always bails out the piper if he gets into difficulties. Hence Bauer and Yamey very reasonably add that paying the cost of wrong decisions will tend to ensure that people "explore opportunities with care before committing their resources, whether labour, land or capital." If all who support community development would clearly agree that "the waste resulting from mistaken decisions [should] fall primarily on those who made the mistake", community development would be taken more seriously in Canada. Nor is this contrary to the principle of justice or fair play.

APPENDIX I

*Religious Denominations of the Indian Population by Province
Departmental Census 1959*

Province or Territory	Anglican	Baptist	United Church	Presbyterian	Roman Catholic	Other Christian Denominations	Aboriginal	Not Stated	All Denominations
P.E.I.	—	—	—	—	340	—	—	1	341
N.S.	—	—	6	—	3,531	2	—	22	3,561
N.B.	—	—	1	—	3,022	—	—	160	3,183
Que.	3,952	5	784	2	14,827	219	215	449	20,455
Ont.	12,232	2,865	6,836	892	14,734	674	2,501	1,934	42,668
Man.	6,999	—	5,899	1,025	9,126	306	82	221	23,658
Sask.	6,915	54	2,015	366	12,462	59	1,170	239	23,280
Alta.	2,436	143	2,127	26	13,853	437	58	207	19,287
B.C.	6,900	—	6,852	—	21,077	1,117	—	277	36,229
Yukon	1,331	93	—	6	438	—	—	6	1,868
N.W.T.	778	—	—	1	3,553	—	—	266	4,598
	41,543	3,160	24,520	2,318	96,963	2,814	4,026	3,782	179,128

Libraries for Indian Communities[1]

At the round-table discussion on community library services for Indians, held in Toronto on May 30, it soon became clear that three kinds of communities, with entirely different sets of problems, were being discussed. The first group, most largely represented at the meeting, were those reserve communities which know that they want libraries, some of whom have taken steps to get them started, and all of whom have encountered difficulties. The second kind of communities are those where the need for a library is not yet felt. That situation may be the result of apathy or of poverty so abysmal that survival needs are completely absorbing. The third community consists of those Indians living in cities or towns who want to use books, or should be stimulated to use them, but who find conventional library facilities forbidding, difficult and unsuited to their needs.

Indians living on reservations who know that they want libraries want to be able to develop them *themselves*, not to have them prefabricated and handed out. But they need help with the technical problems involved. This was the distinct impression made by the various personal reports given at the round table. On the Six Nations Reserve in Ohsweken, Ontario, a Public Library Board has been recognized and encouraged by the Band Council. The initiative to get the Board set up was taken by members of the local Women's Institute. The Board has been offered a building but it would have to be moved to a different site and there is a question whether it is worth moving and repairing. A large number of books which have been donated remain in storage. The Public Library Board has orga-

[1] Reprinted by courtesy of the Indian-Eskimo Association of Canada from its *Bulletin*, September 1965.

nized fund-raising events but they have not been able to find out through their superintendent how to go about securing from any outside source, like the province or Indian Affairs Branch, the substantial funds necessary to start operating. "We feel we are being held back from being a self-reliant people," said one member of the Board.

Similar frustrations are being experienced at Walpole Island where the Band has set up a Library and Museum Committee which has made considerable progress. The Band has allocated funds and members have donated labour to make necessary repairs to a building acquired from the federal government. They have purchased supplies such as tables, chairs, shelving. Now their great need is for help with cataloguing the books and training one or more of their members to look after their circulation. Appeals to the province and a nearby library had elicited no offers of help.

Other communities have some books but no place to put them. At Cape Croker, for example, they want a community centre and plan to put a room in it for a library. At present they are waiting for funds to get started on the centre.

In Saskatchewan a new system of regional libraries is being set up which will make it possible for reserves to have library services where there is sufficient desire on the part of the Indians. The province will consider the reserves as municipalities for this purpose and will contribute 75 cents per person toward this end plus an initial grant of $1.50 per person for the purchase of books. The Band must match the 75 cent grant. . . .

From these particular instances it is possible to make some generalizations about the problems facing any Band members who can persuade their Band Council that they really want a library.

First they must make a realistic appraisal of how they expect it to be used and what resources they have already at hand. If there is a school on the reserve, there are presumably some library facilities for the children. It might be possible to expand these. . . . If a new school or community centre is being built, it might be possible to request that a room be provided for a library. Ideally the library should be as useful and attractive to adults as to children and should be for the use of the whole family. As adult education is stressed more and more, adults too will need reference books and a place to study.

One kind of practical help that all libraries need is in the training of staff. Nobody knows how to run a library by instinct. There is a great need for more short courses and opportunities for in-service training. These can be arranged under the various training and adult education schemes operated by the Indian Affairs Branch and some of the provinces. . . .

. . . . .

NOTE

Since the above article was published, the Department of Indian Affairs has appointed a Supervisor of Library Services, who is attached to the Education Division and who has begun the business of trying to help Band Councils meet the needs set out in the article. Accordingly, since November, 1966, Band Councils can authorize the setting up of a library, delegating responsibility to a board which collects information on the library needs of the local Indians and which appoints as a librarian someone who is familiar with the local community and is ready to be trained for a librarian's job. Other assistants may be employed or contribute voluntary service, to help with clerical work, lead discussion groups, run film showings, etc. The Band's job is to consult with provincial and regional library officials about how the library may be developed.

It should, of course, be understood that this development still depends not only on the local activity of the Indian population but upon the willingness of provincial library authorities to co-operate and to treat Bands as municipalities for library purposes. This may be one of the points at which public pressure may need to be applied in support of the efforts of the Federal Supervisor of Library Services by the non-Indian population of each province.

Select List of Books, Periodicals, Films and Filmstrips

1. ON CHURCH MISSIONS TO CANADIAN INDIANS AND ESKIMOS

ANGLICAN CHURCH OF CANADA

Head Office: Church House, 600 Jarvis Street, Toronto 5, Ontario.

Books:

Boon, T. C. B., *The Anglican Church from the Bay to the Rockies.* Toronto, Ryerson Press, 1962.

Carrington, Philip, *The Anglican Church in Canada: A History.* Toronto, Collins, 1963.

Cody, H. A., *An Apostle of the North: Memoirs of the Rt. Rev. William Carpenter Bompas.* London, Seely, 1908.

Collison, W. H., *In the Wake of the War Canoe.* London, Seeley, Service, 1915.

Fleming, A. L., *Archibald the Arctic.* New York, Appleton-Century-Crofts, 1956.

Gould, Sydney, *Inasmuch: Sketches of the Beginnings of the Church of England in Canada in Relation to the Indian and Eskimo Races.* Toronto, Missionary Society of the Church of England in Canada, 1917.

Kellaway, W., *The New England Company, 1649-1776; Missionary Society to the American Indians.* London, Longmans, 1961.

Peake, F. A., *The Bishop Who Ate His Boots.* Toronto, Anglican Church of Canada, 1966.

Renison, R. J., *One Day at a Time: Autobiography.* Toronto, Kingswood House, 1957.

Periodicals:

Arctic News. The Diocese of the Arctic, 1055 Avenue Road, Toronto 12, Ontario.

BAPTIST CHURCH

Head Office: Baptist Federation of Canada, 91 Queen Street, Brantford, Ontario.

Books:

From Sea to Sea. Toronto, The Women's Baptist Home Mission Board of Ontario West, 1940.

PRESBYTERIAN CHURCH IN CANADA

Head Office: 50 Wynford Drive, Don Mills, Ontario.

Books and Pamphlets:

Andrews, J. Eldon, *The Canadian Indian: Towards a Better Understanding.* Toronto, Missionary Education Committee, 1966.

MacNab, John, *They Went Forth.* Toronto, McClelland and Stewart, 1933.

————*In Other Tongues.* Toronto, The Thorn Press, 1939.

The Story of Our Missions. Toronto, Women's Missionary Society, The Presbyterian Church in Canada, 1915.

ROMAN CATHOLIC CHURCH

Head Office for Indian and Eskimo Work: Indian and Eskimo Welfare Commission of the Oblate Fathers, 238 Argyle Ave., Ottawa 4.

Books:

Champagne, Joseph-Etienne, *Les Missions Catholiques dans l'Ouest Canadien.* Editions de l'Université d'Ottawa, 1949.

Duchaussois, Pierre, *Mid Snow and Ice.* Ottawa University, 1937.

————*Hidden Apostles* (trans. Fr. Thomas Dawson), Dublin, Lourdes Messenger Office, 1937.

Parkman, Francis, *The Jesuits in North America in the Seventeenth Century.* Boston, Little, Brown, 1879 (out of print).

Periodicals:

Oblate News, 2015 West 8th Ave., Vancouver, B.C.

Eskimo, published by Oblate Missions, Churchill, Man.

UNITED CHURCH OF CANADA

Head office: 83 St. Clair Ave. East, Toronto 7, Ontario.

Books and Pamphlets:

Birch Bark Talking—A Resumé of the Life and Work of the Rev. James Evans. Toronto, published by the Board of Home Missions, 1940.

Commission to Study Indian Work. Toronto, published by the Board of Home Missions, 1958.

MacDonald, M.C., *From Lakes to Northern Lights.* Toronto, United Church Publishing House, 1951.

MacLean, J., *McDougall of Alberta.* Toronto, Ryerson Press, 1927.

————*Vanguards of Canada.* (The many short biographical studies include those on Kahkewayquonaby, Chief Joseph, R. T. Rundle, Thomas Crosby and Henry B. Steinhauer.) Toronto, United Church Publishing House, 1918.

Nix, J. E., *Mission Among the Buffalo—The Work of the McDougalls in the Canadian Northwest, 1860-1876.* Toronto, Ryerson Press, 1960.

Playter, G. F., *The History of Methodism in Canada, with an Account*

of the Rise and Progress of the Work of God Among the Canadian
Indian Tribes. Toronto, Anson, Green, 1862 (out of print).

Scott, R. C., My Captain Oliver. Toronto, United Church Publishing
House, 1947.

Shipley, Nan, Anna and the Indians—The Work of Mrs. S. D. Gaudin.
Toronto, Ryerson Press, 1966.

———The James Evans Story. Toronto, Ryerson Press, 1966.

2. OF IMPORTANCE FOR A GENERAL STUDY

Canada, Indian Affairs Branch, The Canadian Indian: A Reference Paper.
Ottawa (most recent re-issue).

Mealing, S. R. (ed.), The Jesuit Relations and Allied Documents: A Selection.
Ottawa, The Carleton Library, No. 7, 1963.

Hawthorn, H. B., et al., The Indians of British Columbia. Toronto, University
of Toronto Press, 1958.

Iglauer, Edith, The New People. New York, Doubleday, 1966.

Jenness, Eileen, The Indian Tribes of Canada. Toronto, Ryerson Press, 1966.

Lagasse, J. H., et al., The People of Indian Ancestry in Manitoba. Winnipeg,
Department of Agriculture and Immigration, Government of Manitoba,
1959.

Leechman, D., The Native Tribes of Canada. Toronto, Gage, 1957.

Loram, C. T., and T. W. McIlwraith (eds.), Seminar-Conference on the North
American Indian Today. Toronto, University of Toronto Press, 1939.

LaViolette, F. A., The Struggle for Survival: Indian Cultures and the Protestant Ethic in British Columbia. Toronto, University of Toronto Press,
1961.

Morris, Sir Alexander, The Treaties of Canada. Toronto, Belfords, Clarke,
1880 (out of print).

Wilson, Edmund, Apologies to the Iroquois. New York, Farrar, Straus and
Cudahy, 1960.

The following publications from the Queen's Printer, Ottawa, are important:
The Indian Act (1951), R.S.C. 1952, c. 149; as amended by 1952-53, c. 41, and
1956, c. 40.

Minutes of Proceedings and Evidence: Joint Committee of the Senate and
the House of Commons on Indian Affairs, 1960-61.

Annual Reports of the Indian Affairs Branch (especially Report for the
Fiscal Year ended March 31, 1965, containing report on the first Federal-
Provincial Ministerial Conference on Indian Affairs, at Ottawa, October
29-30, 1964).

Also important are the following publications of the Indian-Eskimo Asso-
ciation of Canada, Toronto:
Education for What?, December, 1965.
The Development of Indian and Eskimo Art and Crafts in the Far North.
May, 1965.

For reference, the following should be consulted:

Anthropologica (Journal of the Centre for Anthropological Research, University of Ottawa), "Indian Education Today", P. André Renaud, November, 1958.

Vallée, F. G., *Sociological Research in the Arctic*. Ottawa, Northern Co-ordination and Research Centre, Department of Northern Affairs and National Resources, 1963.

3. RELEVANT TO INDIAN AND ESKIMO FOLKLORE

Barbeau, C. M., *The Indian Speaks*. Toronto, Macmillan, 1943.

————*The Tree of Dreams*. Toronto, Oxford University Press, 1955.

Clark, E. E., *Indian Legends of Canada*. Toronto, McClelland and Stewart, 1960.

Houston, James, *Tikta' Liktak*. New York, Harcourt, 1966.

4. CONCERNING SOME OUTSTANDING INDIANS

Chalmers, H., and E. B. Monture, *Joseph Brant, Mohawk*. Toronto, Ryerson Press, 1955.

Monture, E. B., *Famous Indians*. Toronto, Clarke Irwin, 1960.

Wood, K., *The Great Chief*. Toronto, Macmillan, 1960.

NATIONAL FILM BOARD FILMSTRIPS

All filmstrips are in colour, except those marked *

Eskimo Carvings (11032)
Eskimo Prints (36128)
Eskimo Sculpture (36124)
Haida Argilite Carvings (11080)*
Indian Rock Paintings (31000)
Indian Snowshoes (937030)
Masks of the North American Indians (37033)
Pauline Johnson (31034)
Totem Poles of the West Coast (17037)*
A Day in the Life of an Indian Boy (937041)
A Day in the Life of an Indian Girl (937040)
Eskimo Children on Baffin Island, Part I (36070)
Eskimo Children on Baffin Island, Part II (36071)

NATIONAL FILM BOARD FILMS

Age of the Beaver, 16 min. 47 sec., black and white, 1951.
Because They Are Different, 27 min. 58 sec., black and white, 1964.
Circle of the Sun, 29 min. 13 sec., colour, 1960.
The Longhouse People, 23 min. 2 sec., colour, 1964.
Peoples of the Skeena, 14 min. 7 sec., colour, 1949.

Index